50

More Ways
To Sell Smarter

Jim Meisenheimer

A Helbern Book

Helbern
Published by the Helbern Group
Libertyville, Illinois 60048, U.S.A.

Helbern Group, Registered Offices:
Libertyville, Illinois

First Helbern Printing, June 1996
10 9 8 7 6 5 4 3 2 1

Copyright © Jim Meisenheimer, 1996

Printed in the United States of America

Library of Congress Catalogue Card Number: 96-075265

ISBN 0-9637479-1-6

In Memory Of John Stevens

An abundance of talent,
a shortage of time.

Contents

#1

Ben - Thanks For The Wake-Up Call

Most salespeople, if given a choice, would not select life insurance as a product to sell. The usual jokes, the reputation of the industry, and the fact that it's been around so long, would not lead salespeople to think they could really make it big in that business.

You couldn't tell that to Ben Feldman though. Ben was eighty-one when he died November 7, 1993. He started selling life insurance just before World War II. The rest as they say is history. He almost single-handedly changed the insurance industry. He was just a salesman.

It's been said that he didn't look like a salesman, didn't sound like a salesman, and didn't act like a salesman. Ben was different in every imaginable way.

Here's some background on Ben Feldman. He was born to Russian, Jewish immigrants that settled in eastern Ohio. At his father's insistence he dropped out of school to sell eggs for $10 a week. He met Fritzie Zaremburg, a teacher, who later became his wife.

After selling insurance to all his friends and relatives, he then targeted businesses in eastern Ohio and western Pennsylvania. Without going beyond a sixty mile radius, he often sold more insurance in a day than most agents would sell in a year. In the 1970's it was reported that he personally sold more insurance than 1,500 of the largest 1,800 life insurance companies.

During his lifetime, he sold insurance policies with a face value over $1.5 billion. One-third of it was sold after he turned sixty-five.

According to many, Ben wasn't ordinary - he was extraordinary. Harry Hohn, Chairman of New York Life said, "Ben really felt everyone in the world was underinsured."

He believed passionately in his product.

Ben knew how to really WOW his customers. His words were his craft. According to Rick Hampson, an AP writer, "He'd sit up late, crafting the pithy sayings that he called power phrases and rehearse them with a tape recorder."

He knew perfection came from practice.

He achieved one goal after another. In 1975 he was the first salesperson to sell $2 million in a single week.

He was goal focused.

"He sold life insurance by talking about life, not death. People didn't die, they walked out, as in, when you walk out, the money walks in - the insurance money," according to Rick Hampson. Taped inside the front cover of his presentation binder were a $1,000 bill and several pennies. He would tell his customers, "For these," pointing to the pennies, "you can get this" - the bill.

He was creative.

In 1992, New York Life created an insurance selling contest they called "Feldman's February." The program was to commemorate his fifty years of selling life insurance. The national contest was of course in honor of Ben's history with the company. Apparently no one told that to Ben. He viewed it as a challenge and won the contest himself. He was eighty and in a hospital recovering from a cerebral hemorrhage during the month of February. That February, he sold $15,150,000 worth of insurance from his hospital bed.

He never gave up.

He never, never, never, never gave up.

Listen to some of Ben's phrases and how his words worked magic. Imagine hearing them as you consider making a decision to buy insurance.

"No one ever died with too much money."

"Do you know anyone who has a lease on life? It isn't a question of if; it's a question of when."

"Put me on your payroll. The day you walk out, I'll walk in and pay your bills."

"The key to a sale is an interview, and the key to an interview is a disturbing question."

"Most people buy not because they believe, but because the salesperson believes."

3

For Ben, success wasn't fleeting, it was a staple. He loved his product. He loved his customers. He loved his company. He loved his work.

Here's a disturbing question. If Ben Feldman sold for your company, how would he do it?

Ben's gone now. His legacy, however, should serve as an inspiration to all that call sales a profession. Ben Feldman gave new meaning to an old profession. Thanks Ben, for the wake up call.

> **Creativity involves taking what you have, where you are, and getting the most out of it.**
> **Carl Mays**

> **Be like a postage stamp. Stick to something until you get it.**
> **Josh Billings**

> **Attitudes are caught, not taught.**
> **Elwood Chapman**

> **One of the major factors which differentiates creative people from lesser creative people is that creative people pay attention to their small ideas.**
> **Roger von Oech**

#2

How To Be Aimless

Why do so many salespeople spend too little time planning, setting, and trying to achieve very specific goals? The excuses are always the same.

■ My goals are in my head.

■ My goals keep changing.

■ What if I don't achieve them?

■ I don't have time to do them.

Perhaps, after reading about Ben Feldman, you may want to reconsider your options. Instead of offering up some ideas on how to become goal-oriented, I thought I'd consider this approach.

Here are three ideas on how to become aimless. By adhering to these three guidelines you can assure yourself of becoming "more of the same" oriented. To remain aimless in life and in your profession - just follow these three steps.

1. Be specifically general in everything you purposefully set out to achieve. Don't imagine aiming at a target, instead see yourself aiming for a blank wall. It's safer

5

and you needn't cross the line in the sand called "risk."

2. Keep all goals in your head. Do not under any circumstances commit them to writing. You give yourself tremendous leeway to change your goals (dreams) when they're not in writing. When you go on vacation, however, it is a good idea to write that list of all those important things that need to get completed before you go away. Write lists for vacations. Don't write lists for your life.

3. Make all goals (dreams) timeless. The best way to achieve something is to give yourself the luxury of unlimited time. Why burden yourself with time frames and target dates. It's more exciting to have important things happen spontaneously and unexpectedly. The world already has too much pressure. Why put more on yourself?

If the choice is really between being goal-focused and aimless, which will you choose? How would you like to be known by the goals you never accomplished?

> **No wind makes for him that hath no intended port to sail unto.**
> **Montaigne**

#3

The World's Finest Video

As you read the headline, you're probably expecting a sales pitch for one of my video tapes, right? Well, sorry to disappoint you. Actually, the best video tape money can buy is not a tape of me, it's a tape of you. Let me explain.

Two years ago, while preparing for a major presentation to a large health care firm, I got nervous. It wasn't as though a large black shadow had been cast over me, it was because I knew that my presentation needed some additional work.

Since this was an especially large group and because this was my first assignment with the company, I was under pressure to create a good first impression with the audience.

I started to HOPE that my approach would be the right one. I also began thinking about the content, style, and methods I was planning to use. You could say that I was developing a severe case of self-doubt.

Whenever self-doubt sets in, I force myself to recall the days when I was a teenager and was absolutely terrified by the thought of having to say something standing up in front of a group. I can't really pinpoint where I developed this fear, but I can pinpoint how I got rid of it.

As an R.O.T.C. student in college I was forced, as a requirement of the military science courses, to prepare and deliver twenty minute lesson plans on the art of military tactics. I was so overtaken with fear, I found myself preparing and practicing my assignments more than I had ever prepared for anything else in my life. And, of course, a funny thing happened.

My worst fears were never realized. In fact, after several opportunities standing up and presenting military logistics to my classmates, I began to look forward to future presentations. I quickly discovered that preparation was an excellent way to combat fear. Not only did preparation minimize my fears, it also provided an incredible boost to my self confidence. For me, preparation and practice are always the two best ways to build confidence.

It's hard to believe that was twenty-eight years ago. Practice then consisted mostly of repetition and working in front of a tall mirror. Now, many years later I was faced with the same familiar anxiety that I'd experienced years earlier. Certainly, preparation and practice would come to my rescue again, only this time I would beef it up with high technology.

Is there any bigger critic of us than ourselves? Of course not. To help me prepare for this presentation I bought a tripod and mounted my video camcorder camera on it. Practice took on a whole new dimension. Preparing and practicing in front of the camera gave me a chance to see what the audience would see, before they actually saw it. The camera doesn't allow you to hide. The film gave me a chance to hear what I was saying, observe how I was saying it, and enabled me to chisel out all the little things that didn't contribute to a strong and dynamic presentation.

I feel the best when I prepare the most.

What's the impact of previewing your skills on video tape? Imagine listening to your every word while seeing your facial expressions and other non-verbal body language. As a sales professional, how can you risk not seeing what your customers see on a daily basis? Every attempt at self-improvement has an immeasurable impact on your personal self-confidence.

Here's a recommended action plan. This plan will get results and increase your confidence. First, answer this question: When it comes to selling, what's your weakest area? Once identified, you're well on your way.

You might feel that cold-calling on the telephone needs work. It could be your open-ended questions. Perhaps you tend to talk features instead of benefits. Maybe you could deal with the price objection more effectively. Asking for the order can be tricky for many of us. Whatever it is, remember to start with your weaknesses not with your strengths. Incremental improvement in your weak areas will become your catalyst to soaring success.

Instinctively, most of us will try to strengthen our strong points. I guess we feel less vulnerable that way. What I'm suggesting is that you pick your soft spot and begin working on it using a camera to record the process of improvement.

Here's the plan:

- Identify your improvement area.

- Outline your current approach on paper.

- Revise your approach on paper.

- Practice on camera for three to five minutes.

- Play it back twice.

- Play it back with the volume off.

- Pay close attention to body language.

- Repeat the process until you nail it down.

- Save your first video to compare.

- Note specific improvements on paper.

- Validate your progress using affirmations.

When it came to my presentation, I was ready. I was filled with enthusiasm and confidence because of the extra preparation and practice. The road to discovery is the road to recovery. There's only one person responsible for self-improvement and self-development. You will discover more about your skills and become empowered to make quantum changes, if you start watching the world's finest video - a video of yourself.

#4

Knowledge Power

The letters in the word "knowledge" have a special interpretation for salespeople. Why do so many salespeople face rejection as often as they do? To hear sales reps explain it, it's usually because of someone else's low-ball pricing. It really has to do with knowledge. That's the reason. We often get no's because we haven't done our homework. We haven't properly assessed the customer's current situation. We haven't analyzed his preferred communication style, and without fully assessing his wants we often fail to demonstrate our real value.

The knowledge we develop about our customers is in direct proportion to the essence of our success. To know is to win. To assume is simply not enough to get even close.

Knowledge of an account, the key decision-makers, their customers, their issues and challenges, position us in an extraordinary way to lock up the account sooner rather than later.

Knowledge also gives us a distinct advantage. Any successful attempt at differentiating our products is totally reliant on our ability to define specific customer requirements. Completely understanding those requirements creates the opportunity for us to demonstrate our unique edge in the marketplace.

Knowledge is power. Learn to leverage the power of your mind. To minimize the no's you get, seek to really know your customers in a way that creates a very personal and very powerful selling edge for you.

> **When you know a thing, to hold that you know it, and when you do not know a thing, to allow that you do not know it: this is knowledge.**
>
> **Confucius**

> **Knowledge is a comfortable and necessary retreat and shelter for us in an advanced age; and if we do not plant it while young, it will give us no shade when we grow old.**
>
> **Lord Chesterfield**

> **I read my eyes out and can't read half enough . . . The more one reads the more one sees we have to read.**
>
> **John Adams**

> **You see, real ongoing, lifelong education doesn't answer questions; it provokes them.**
>
> **Luci Swindoll**

#5

Real World Customer Expectations

A real short definition for the word "customer" is a "patron, buyer, shopper, or a person one has to deal with." Not many salespeople would knowingly treat a customer, especially a good customer, as someone they have to deal with. The key word is knowingly. How many of us do it unwittingly? How many of us know our customers so well, it's virtually impossible not to take them for granted?

Whether you have long-term customer relationships or ones just beginning, here's a little reminder of what most customers expect from professional salespeople.

Customerize everything you do for me - your customer. Remember I can tell the difference between a sales pitch and a presentation that's tailored to my needs and wants. Anything you can do to make me feel special will truly be appreciated since most salespeople handle me like I'm next on their list.

Understand everything there is to know about us. Take the time to get acquainted with our people, our programs, and our policies. Try to understand more about our requirements before you serve up your products as the solution. Taking this extra time to learn more about us demonstrates, more than your words ever will, that you really care.

Specialize in our needs and wants. Talking in generalities won't distinguish you and certainly won't favorably differentiate you and your company.

Trust means never having to say we've made a mistake about you. Trust can't be bought and usually shouldn't be rushed. It appears over time in the form of credibility and consistency in everything we do together. Maybe we'll never see the word "trust" written into one of your contracts, but we'll never expect one without it.

Organize the priorities of our working relationship. Time is our most precious commodity, and our preference is to invest it not waste it. When you call on us, come prepared. Be sure you do your homework. Remember it takes two to have a conversation. Don't be like most salespeople who call on us with the compulsion to do all the talking.

Measure. What gets measured gets done. The key to our mutual success is your ability to define and deliver to exacting standards. Seek to deliver more than you promise, and be sure to monitor your promises.

Energize your sales call. It's amazing how many salespeople we see who aren't genuinely enthusiastic and excited about their products. Enthusiasm is contagious. I can't get excited about your products if you're not.

Relatability is a critical ingredient to a successful working relationship. The people you'll be calling on won't all share your perspective. Some might be more analytical than you. They deserve more details and information than you ordinarily provide. Some of our people are real doers. They want things done yesterday. Some of our people are the thinkers and planners in our company.

They want to know all the reasons why you are making specific recommendations. Relating to our diverse group may be your most challenging and important task.

As you can see, the short definition for the word "customer" won't win many trophies around here. The long version will.

> **Customer service in America stinks.**
>
> **Tom Peters**

> **Quality in a service or product is not what you put into it. It is what the customer gets out of it.**
>
> **Peter Drucker**

> **Service is just a day-in, day-out, ongoing, never-ending, unremitting, persevering, compassionate type of activity.**
>
> **Leon Gorman**

> **There is only one boss. The customer. And he can fire everybody in the company from the chairman on down, simply by spending his money somewhere else.**
>
> **Sam Walton**

> **The individual (the customer) perceives service in his or her own terms.**
>
> **Arch McGill**

#6

Make Power Calls

The key to creating more telephone income opportunities is to form a new habit using a professional telephone presentation for all business-related calls. Many sales-people skilled at delivering powerful face-to-face sales presentations rely on old personal telephone habits when making business telephone calls.

For a salesperson, the telephone is a powerful tool. If the proper techniques are used the opportunities are limitless, especially with the increasing popularity of car and cellular phones.

There are three essential steps in making effective telephone presentations. The first is to know your objective. This may sound simplistic, but if you don't know the objective how can you possibly achieve it? Simply stated, you should know the purpose of every business call before you reach for the phone.

Once the objective is clearly understood, your second step is to prepare your delivery by focusing your content on the objective. Naturally, anything that doesn't contribute to the objective shouldn't be used during the conversation. The key to focused content is preparation, preparation, and preparation.

The third step in making successful business calls is to aim for clarity and brevity. Try avoiding all those big four syllable words and use simple language that is easily understood. If time is money, shouldn't you invest it wisely, even on the telephone? Brevity allows you to make more calls.

The verbal picture you create is important so consider these reminders when making a professional call. Be sure they can hear your smile. Be positive throughout the call. Be enthusiastic. Be prepared to succeed.

The right word may be effective, but no word was ever as effective as a rightly timed pause.

Mark Twain

An intellectual is a man who takes more words than necessary to tell more than he knows.

Dwight D. Eisenhower

Talk low, talk slow, and don't say too much.

John Wayne

#7

Whacko Self Re-Newal Ideas

1. Take a fun break every day. Is there any chance you're taking your job too seriously lately? If you're like most salespeople, you've got more to do than time to get it done. So, do we grin and bear it, or is it easier to tense up and worry more? Imagine you're on your death bed. Is it conceivable that you would regret not being more serious? Not a chance. Don't let a day go by where you don't schedule some fun. Read the comics, sing a song, read a poem, call a friend, or even play a practical joke or two. Learn to lighten up; take it from a serious person, it's not easy but it's worth the effort.

2. Do spring cleaning year-round. Professionalism can't be sustained in a cluttered environment. The three candidates for routine clutter busters are your office, your car and your briefcase. There's no easy way to do it only a simple way. Get the largest trash can liner you can find and get rid of everything that isn't absolutely essential. Don't worry about trashing something you might need later, someone else will have it.

3. Plan a retreat (annually). I know. You think I've lost it. You barely have enough time to do the really important things. Try this quick experiment. Stand as close to a wall as you can. Consider the wall as your job. When you're standing that close what happens to

your perspective? It's been said that distance creates perspective. To gain new insight, take a step back to capture a perspective that will move you forward in a refreshed way. Any place will do, as long as it's not one you're familiar with. It's a good idea, just do it!

4. Change the look of things. Now this will take guts. It requires changing some things. Empty your briefcase. Reorganize it so it looks different. Move things around in your office. Place the waste basket on the other side of your desk. Move the in basket. If you want to keep up with a changing world, you have to thrive on change. Changing the little things can often have a big impact. Really, if you can't make the little changes, what makes you think you are making the big ones.

5. Start a success journal. This isn't a diary - so guys, don't get turned off. Start off by getting a composition notebook. You remember, the speckled black and white version. Write "Success Journal" on the cover. Use it for developing new ideas, recording successes, or adding articles that relate to your business. Here's what happens. At first you have a success journal. After a short while, if you're like me, it'll become a resource journal. I wouldn't be without mine; I'll bet you won't want to be without yours either.

6. Give mini "Oscar's." It's no secret that we are starved for recognition. Each one of us every day has the opportunity to recognize the efforts of those around us who in some small yet significant way helps us achieve our personal goals. To give recognition is no big thing, to get it is. Simple things work best - a handwritten note, a bottle of wine, a memo with a copy to the boss or even a telephone call that just

says "thanks." Don't let a week go by without giving at least one "Oscar."

7. Get a mentor. Look up the word "mentor" in the dictionary. Then find a person that fits that description. A mentor can help you model the right behaviors.

8. Ignite your spirit. Remember, motivation is an inside job. Each one of us possesses an inner flame that flickers and shines brightly. Your mind is the fuel that adjusts your passion and enthusiasm. To keep the burners turned on, stay focused, think - "yes I can" and never, never, never, never give up.

> **Keep polishing, for the minute you stop, the brass starts to tarnish.**
> **Stanley Marcus**
> **Neiman-Marcus Department Store**

> **If you have a dream, give it a chance to happen.**
> **Richard de Vos**

> **Take your mind out every now and then and dance on it. It is getting all caked up.**
> **Mark Twain**

#8

"For You"

How many times a day do you say the words, "for you?" You might be passing up sales opportunities considering the power these words have. A restaurant recently experimented with these words. They asked the service staff to incorporate these words throughout the dining experience as often as possible.

Imagine your cocktails, the menu, a wine list, fresh ground pepper, dinner rolls, the dessert tray, and even coffee being served and accompanied with the words "for you." There is something special about these words if said sincerely.

During a sales training seminar in August 1994, I asked a group of salespeople to develop a list of statements using the words "for you," as they might be incorporated into a sales call. Most thought it would be easy to do. I guess that's because most of us genuinely believe we're already doing it. Surprise. Surprise. It became a very difficult exercise, taking more time than anyone realized.

If you think it's easy, try writing four or five comments using the words "for you" in a substantive way. My guess is that you'll have to think about it. But, if all it takes is a little thought to sound a lot better - it'll be worth the effort.

P.S. The waiters and waitresses who were involved in the experiment, reported their tips increased over 20% after they started using the words "for you." It's just a thought - I did it "for you."

To serve is beautiful, but only if it's done with joy and a whole heart and a free mind.

Pearl S. Buck

Pressed into service means pressed out of shape.

Robert Frost

Don't worry about profits, worry about service.

Thomas Watson, Sr.

Above all, we wish to avoid having a dissatisfied customer. We consider our customers a part of our organization, and we want them to feel free to make any criticism they see fit in regard to our merchandise or service. Sell practical, tested merchandise at reasonable profit, treat your customers like human beings - and they will always come back.

L.L. Bean

#9

I Think, I Assume, I Don't Know

Building a new house is exciting at best and nightmarish at worst. In my business as a consultant, trainer and speaker, I'm extremely fortunate to be able to work from a home office. So fortunate, in fact, that my wife Bernadette and I decided to include a home office in a vacation home we were building in Sarasota, Florida.

Because of the distance between both homes, all of the work-in-process decisions were made over the phone, using Federal Express, and relying on the FAX. We would receive updates from the builder, in the form of change orders, followed by a request for additional funds. Our real estate salesman, Dick, would routinely send us pictures of the house at key points during construction. It was a nice touch, especially since the builder was not directly affiliated with the real estate developer, and Dick's job was essentially completed.

Though we were in no particular rush and didn't have a deadline, we thought it was prudent to ask the builder for an estimated time-frame for completion. He was very comfortable with October 1st and so were we. At the beginning of September, Bernadette confirmed the target dates once more. We received nothing but reassurances.

We arrived at our new home at 7:00 A.M. on October 6th and immediately went into total shock. We couldn't believe how much still remained to be done. For the next ten days we heard a continuous chorus of "I think, I assume, and I don't know." We heard this from the foreman who greeted us with, "I think we can have this in good shape for you by the end of the day." Later that same day the construction superintendent, who was ready to go on vacation said, "I assume all the subcontractors will be here tomorrow to get things finished for you." Two days later and hours before he was about to depart for a three-week vacation, the builder greeted us with total disbelief when he saw what still needed to be completed. While looking at us and glaring at his construction foreman he uttered the unbelievable words, "I don't know how this happened."

So what's the point of this little war story? Is it to complain about our disappointment? Not really. Is it to point the finger of blame in a particular direction? Not really. In business, as in life, there will always be problems. It would be truly memorable if we could all avoid problems, but the reality is that we can't escape them. The real challenge rests in how we choose to deal with them.

If authority and responsibility are to march hand in hand, they must be accompanied by the right actions. Being tentative, creating distance, casting doubt, becoming evasive, and sounding unprofessional are not ways to handle customers' problems. In this situation Bernadette and I were customers and, because of the way we were treated, we felt our initial trust in the builder had turned into quicksand.

As a professional salesperson, if you ever find yourself in a tenuous situation with a customer, try to imagine what his or her position and feelings are before you attempt to respond. While your actions will always speak louder than your words, your words often create the opportunity to calm, console, and demonstrate to your customers what you're really made of.

Here are several suggestions on how to respond to difficult situations.

"I think" - should never be used. If you're not sure, say "I believe" or "I feel" to express yourself. Another alternative is, "I'd be happy to check that for you."

"I assume" should be avoided at all costs. It's a statement that can make anyone sound like an idiot. "I'd be glad to confirm" is a better alternative.

Steer clear of "I don't know." Why confess to incompetency? Instead make the focus of your response - speed. Emphasize how quickly you can find out. For example, "That's a good question, let me check and get right back to you."

The best way to deal effectively with customers' problems is to avoid any tactics that delay, deflect, or defer the issues being raised. The most sensible approach is to be factual, direct, and sensitive to the people involved and the situation at hand. Most folks are less concerned about the problems than they are with the practical solutions. Always remember to treat people the way they want to be treated, not the way you want to be treated. They may not share your taste in treatment.

#10

Getting Ready To Sell More

If your first reaction is to ask how you can sell more, be prepared to work hard. Selling is easy if you work real hard at it; ask any successful salesperson. If selling more were really that easy, wouldn't everybody be doing it? You bet they would, but of course you realize that a majority of professional salespeople never soar to the heights of success they are capable of.

Here are a few reminders. If you want to be remembered, you must be different. Nobody remembers plain vanilla. There are three things you can differentiate: you, your products, and your company. If you can answer this question, "How specifically are you, your services, and your company different?" you are well on your way to differentiation. If you can't spell out these differences, you may be guilty of being vanilla.

Vanilla gets to be chocolate-fudge-ripple by adding flavoring and extra ingredients. What are you adding to your selling repertoire? Make sure you know how your services and company are different from your competition. When it comes to making a real difference, "you" are the most essential extra ingredient. What you can do that is different is limited only by your own creativity and imagination.

Take Fred who sells pet food and supplies to local stores. He suggested to the owners that they offer a free photo with Santa to all their loyal customers. If the owners could get an employee to play Santa, Fred would supply the Christmas gifts. Fred got his company to run a bundle of tree-shaped doggy treats which were packaged and tied with a bow. He also supplied some cardboard frames with the logo of the food company. Some store owners went all out creating little stage areas with Santa on a throne topped by an arbor of pine boughs. Pet lovers showed up with their Rovers and Fifis, received a Polaroid of their beloved which was slipped in the frame, and got a cheery "Merry Christmas" as they were given their doggy goodies. Not only did Fred increase his sales, he also helped his customers increase their sales.

Tom had been submitting proposal after proposal to a soft-drink company trying to get the bid for their labels. One day, he got one of the company's bottles, rolled his proposal into a tight scroll and slipped it into the bottle. He made a mock-up of the label on his computer and glued it to the bottle. The company's slogan was printed and put into the lining of the cap. As a finishing touch, the bottle was gift-wrapped and delivered to his contact. Tom wound up with the company's business.

Hank owns a chain of pizza restaurants. Much of his business is in home delivery. Since he has many teens working for him, he knows mistakes will be made. Hank spends time training all his drivers and managers. When the wrong pizza shows up at a house, the driver is instructed to call the restaurant. The right pizza is immediately dispatched to the house. Along with the right order is a hand-written note apologizing for the mistake and a free six-pack of soda. Hank's managers report that they have more calls thanking them for the soda and commenting on what a nice touch it was than complaints about the service.

Fred, Tom, and Hank increased sales. People remember them because what they did was different. How to your customers remember you?

> **Creativity is especially expressed in the ability to make connections, to make associations, to turn things around and express them in a new way.**
> **Tim Hansen**

> **Creativity involves taking what you have, where you are, and getting the most out of it.**
> **Carl Mays**

> **Creativity is like a muscle - it has to be stretched and exercised regularly to keep it fit and functioning.**
> **Gloria Hoffman and Pauline Graivier**
> **Speak the Language of Success**

> **Creativity is the natural extension of our enthusiasm.**
> **Earl Nightingale**

#11

How To Listen To Silent Movies

If you ever had the opportunity to watch an old-time silent movie, you'll remember the two principle ways to keep up with action: sub-titles and visual cues.

The sub-titles or printed words appearing on the bottom of the screen helped us understand what was being said. Since we couldn't hear what was being said, we had to rely on our eyes as our main sensory receptor. We learned to listen with our eyes and pay attention to facial and bodily mannerisms.

Today of course, the cinema offers technicolor, quadraphonic sound systems, and a myriad of special effects. We've learned to rely less on visual cues both at the movies and in our daily lives. While it's hard to know for sure, I'll bet we often miss seeing important and revealing gestures when making sales calls.

Nonverbal communication is essentially the art of communicating without words. Without words we would be forced to listen more often with our eyes, just as our grandparents did when watching those silent movies. The more acutely we see things, the better we'll understand our customers.

Here are some examples of common nonverbal communications. Using the space between each example,

29

write down your interpretation of what they mean.

1. Avoids making eye contact with you.

2. Crosses arms on chest. Legs tightly crossed. Grim facial expression.

3. Folding and unfolding the bows of a pair of eyeglasses.

4. Tugging at ear while another talks without stopping.

5. Hands together in a prayer-like gesture. Leaning slightly back from the table in the chair.

6. Hand goes to mouth and covers it partially while speaking.

© *1983 Organization Design and Development, Inc.*

See the next page for the correct interpretations. What could it mean if your interpretations didn't match those of the experts? If we miss these signals, we can add needless time to the selling cycle. When you're face-to-face with your customers be sure to focus your attention on what they are saying and how they are saying it.

An excellent way to improve your nonverbal skills is to order the Nonverbal Sensitivity Indicator developed by Rollin Glaser which includes fifty nonverbal interpretations. The instrument may be ordered from Organization Design and Development, Inc. by calling 800- 633-4533.

Silent movies were so much fun because we became totally involved in seeing. We can have more fun, learn more, and dramatically improve our relationships with customers if we refocus our attention to the sights and the sounds we observe.

Probable meaning to non-verbal cues: 1. The party feels negative toward you and would prefer to limit the interaction. 2. Closed, defensive, suspicious; unreceptive, withdrawn from meaningful discussion. 3. Boredom with the discussion. 4. This person wants to participate in the discussion. 5. This person has a high degree of self-confidence and is certain of what he/she is saying. 6. Gesture suggests self-doubt; uncertainty.

> **The most important thing in communication is to hear what isn't being said.**
> **Peter Drucker**

> **When it comes to body language, there are some who have better vocabularies than others.**
> **Doug Larson**

#12

Characteristics Of
Very Successful Salespeople

Did you ever wonder what successful salespeople are made of? I have. There is nothing ordinary about their success. They always seem to be doing more, or putting something extra into their selling effort. I believe that's what makes really successful salespeople extraordinary.

The following is a list of qualities that seem to cluster around the very best in our profession.

They have clearly defined goals in writing. It's not the writing that achieves the goal; it's the specificity of it. Writing ensures that it gets done. During a recent sales training seminar I gave, a woman said she didn't have to write her goals down because she kept them in her head. I asked her how many goals she had in her head. She couldn't recall. Keeping very specific goals in writing is one of the keys to success. Do this for personal and professional goals and your life will change immediately.

Successful salespeople passionately pursue their goals. What's passion if not focused energy. Once the goal is set, successful salespeople think "yes I can" rather than "yes I can't." The real difference between can and can't is the letter "T" for try. Passionate salespeople enjoy the journey to the destination. They are the ones with the sparkle in their eyes. In the 1994 New York Marathon with only three-quarters of a mile to go, German Silva made a wrong turn. The mistake cost him forty meters and twelve seconds of valuable time. What was his attitude at this potentially low point? He said, "If you haven't crossed the finish line, you have a possibility." He won the race beating Benjamin Paredes by two seconds and the closest finish in New York Marathon history.

Successful salespeople dare to be different. During my seminars when we're discussing company, product, and personal differentiation I always ask the participants, "What makes you different?" Most salespeople respond with empty words and say that it's their experience, knowledge, sincerity, integrity, or follow-up which makes them different. While most of us aspire to gain experience, grow in knowledge, be genuinely sincere, possess integrity, and be good at the follow-up - doing these things doesn't make us different. If we are no different than our competitors, our customers often conclude we're all alike. Whether that becomes a reality or is just a perception, the implication is the same. The primary concern of customers, when all other things appear to be equal, is of course the dreaded price. Being different is so important that it is absolutely amazing that it's neglected in sales training programs.

Here a real life example of how one salesman carved out his personal differentiation. In this example he is a cutlery sales representative. He calls mostly on large retail stores that carry his line. Sales calls often include thirty minute training programs to the staff conducted usually before the store opens. So far there's nothing different, right? Wrong! Once a year he offers the staff a complimentary tail-gate lunch served in the mall parking lot. The lunch is prepared and served with, you guessed it, his line of housewares and cutlery.

Remember, if you want to make a difference, you gotta be different. How, specifically, do you differentiate yourself from your competitors.

Successful salespeople have positive attitudes - they always expect the best. Easy to say and hard to do. Successful people aren't immune to the daily swings in day-to-day living. Successful people aren't easily derailed from their mission as professional salespeople. When they experience a negative situation, they refuse to wear it as a badge of discouragement. Instead they focus their attention on their prospects and customers who have their own problems to be solved. If I could sum it up in one word, it would be "showtime." Whenever really successful salespeople make sales calls they turn it "on." They'll dig deep. They're ready and they're on in front of all prospects and customers.

To help them along this highway of positive attitudes, successful salespeople will rely on personal affirmations. Affirmations are the words we use in self-talk communications. An example is "Every day in every way, I'm getting better and better." Imagine how you'd feel saying that twenty-five times a day, every day. They also rely on the mirror. Before every call they check to insure they are wearing a smile instead of a frown.

Your current attitude begins with a thought. Each of us chooses our thoughts. Each day we move closer to our dominant thoughts. For negative thinkers, this is a curse. For the positive thinkers, this becomes a real blessing. Be sure to make your dominant thoughts positive ones, especially when you're surrounded by negative temptations.

Successful salespeople view themselves as students of selling instead of masters of selling. You'll seldom hear a top-of-the-heap salesperson boast "I've always done it this way." The simple truth is, that's because they are always changing, fine-tuning, and adjusting their methods. The super-sellers realize, more than the platoons of mediocrity, that to sustain real success they must make continuous change a part of their daily selling routine.

How this perpetual change manifests itself, of course, will vary individually. Some will read the right stuff like <u>Selling Power</u> magazine (800-752-7355). Some will regularly buy and read books. Buying and reading are not synonymous. Recent surveys reveal that a significant percentage of books purchased never get read. Buying books makes some people feel better simply because they own them. Knowledge cannot be consumed via osmosis, at least not in the foreseeable future.

The real professionals are likely to have manila folders for each of these topics: negotiating, time management, sales planning, communication skills, listening, organization, presentation skills, prospecting, telephone skills, features and benefits, questioning, handling concerns, asking for the business, how to follow-up, and even a folder on neuro-linguistic programming. Whenever they read or scan an article about these topics, it gets filed. Imagine the resources they possess just over a short span of time. The impact on competence and confidence is geometric.

It's always been said that selling is easy if you work hard at it. Success correlates to work. Results come from focused efforts. The thing I respect most about success is that it comes from sustained personal growth. With personal growth you get everything you want.

#13

What's Out . . . What's In

Peddling	Building relationships
Persuading - convincing	Helping and understanding
Talking too much	Acute listening
Ducks	Eagles
Sales strategies	Customer strategies
Me (focus)	You (focus)
More of the same	Radical self-engineering
Transactional sales	Evolving relationships
Closer	Partner
Nickel and diming	Inclusive wrap-a-round service
Know-it-all	Learn-it-all
Double talk	Technobabble
Daytimers	ACT

Old style communications	Information superhighway
Motivational speakers	Edu-tainers
High tech	High touch
FAX numbers	Internet numbers
Rolodex cards	Rolodex software
In-baskets	E-mail
Telephones	Videophones
Yellow pages	Web pages

Change alone is eternal, perpetual,
immortal.

Arthur Schopenhauer

Change is happening faster than we can
keep tabs on it and threatens to shake the
foundations of the most secure American
business.

U.S. Congress, Office of Technology

If you thought it yesterday, if you're
thinking it today, you won't think it
tomorrow.

Faith Popcorn, The Popcorn Report

#14

Ask And You Will Receive

In his book, <u>Winning With The Power Of Persuasion</u>, Joseph Mancuso indicated the most powerful three letter word is the word "ask." He also said that most children ask about sixty questions a day. After they graduate from college, they're asking two questions a day and one of them is "When do we eat?" His words got me thinking.

I remember being a teenager. The two things I feared the most were asking girls to dance and having to get up and speak to groups. When it came to asking girls to dance, I don't recall what I was afraid of, especially since I liked to dance. I was probably imagining that those three pimples located prominently on my chin would turn into eight even bigger ones.

If only I could do it all over again. I realize I can't. But if only I could, here's what I'd do. Being a teenager about thirteen or fourteen, I still wouldn't be driving a car but I would have a bike. I would get on that bike and ride and practice, ride and practice. I would practice exactly what I wanted to say to the girl I wanted to dance with. I'd say it out loud so I could feel the words.

The night of the dance I would feel great. Actually, I'd feel like a pillar of competence and a tower of confidence. And do you know why? Of course it's because I practiced exactly what I was going to say. There would be no hesitation in my voice as I walked up to the girl I wanted to dance with and said, "I like to dance fast and I like to dance slow, which do you prefer?"

When I use this story in seminars, I like to remind people that what made me nervous as a kid was the fear of rejection.

When I reflect back to those days as a young boy, I now realize that what really created the anxiety for me, was that I didn't know specifically *how* to ask the girls to dance.

If I knew then what I know now - I'd be the King of Dance, at least in my high school.

> **We are all, it seems, saving ourselves for the Senior Prom. But many of us forget that somewhere along the way we must learn to dance.**
>
> **Alan Harrington**

> **Some people wait so long for their ship to come in, their pier collapses.**
>
> **John Goddard**

#15

Make Time To Find Time

Time is a critical resource. The way most folks squander it, you'd think everyone had more than they needed. Why do so many people scream about how much more time they need on the one hand and do so little to manage their time on the other? Managing time is a little like brushing your teeth. It's something you have to do every day, and no one can do it for you.

There are all kinds of systems designed to help you manage your time. There are Day Timers, Franklin Planners, and even Time Systems. Each comes with a lesson on how to use it and a portfolio style book where you are instructed to keep everything except your love letters.

It's not enough to consider time in the traditional day, week, and month framework. To manage your time more wisely, you should view it in smaller increments. Start with fifteen minutes. Most of us think nothing of wasting fifteen minutes. What's fifteen minutes aside from being a small chunk of time? Fifteen minutes is 1% of a twenty-four hour day. Squander fifteen minutes and you've wasted 1% of your day. Waste fifteen minutes and you've blown 3% of a typical workday.

You can't save time like you can money. You can't put fifteen minutes into the cookie jar side-by-side with your loose change. Time can't be saved, it can only be spent. How you spend your time is the real challenge.

It's all about how you value, prioritize, use, fill, plan, control, waste, and squander your precious time. There are 168 hours in a week. When asked, most people don't realize how many hours are in a week unless they do the multiplication. Every increment of your time has value. How you use it will contribute to how you are remembered. Here's some time spending ideas.

■ Invest 1% of each day planning how you will spend the other 99%.

■ Never let a day begin without a written and prioritized list of activities.

■ Do big things first. Start with the tough stuff.

■ Do the math to calculate the value (dollars) of fifteen minutes.

■ If 80% of your sales comes from 20% of your customers - allocate your time accordingly.

■ If 80% of your prospects' potential comes from 20% of your prospects - allocate your time accordingly.

■ Memorize the difference between being efficient and being effective. It's said to be the difference between doing something right and doing the right thing.

■ Always focus on being effective.

■ Before you do anything yourself, consider the value of your time compared to the cost of paying someone else to do it.

■ The difference between having potential and achieving success is the difference between thinking and doing. Success is all about doing. Nike's theme isn't "do it later." It's "do it now."

■ You own your time. Don't permit other people to rob you of your time. When you see time robbers approaching say, "gotta run."

■ Avoid all time traps.

■ Each day read for fifteen minutes about your profession.

We all live by the same clock, it's how we wear the watch that makes the real difference. It's not really about making time, though it is about spending it wisely. If you spend most of your time doing what's really important to you, you will have all the time you ever needed.

Gotta run.

> **Yesterday is a cancelled check. Tomorrow is promissory note. Today is cash in hand; spend it wisely.**
>
> **Kay Lyons**

#16

How To PAVE The Way To Increased Sales

I was recently asked to give a presentation to the Professional Speakers Of Illinois. They wanted me to talk about the impact of technology on small businesses. I took a little poetic license and called my presentation, "How To Double Your Sales Without Quadrupling Your Effort." There was a great deal of interest in the topic, because most people are looking for new and quick formulas for success. I did present several new ideas, though none of them are guaranteed to work overnight.

At least four of the points in that presentation have relevance to sales. In fact they were born in the sales arena. Here they are:

*P*lan. There is no easy road to success. However, success is definitely more elusive to those salespeople who fail to plan. First, few superstar salespeople enjoy planning. Most would prefer to sell. Success in selling comes from doing what we like and doing what is necessary. Planning is an absolute essential to sustaining your sales success. There are two ingredients required for results-oriented planning: pencil and paper, or keyboard and screen. Planning can't be done in your head. If it's not written, it's not a plan. If you can't see it, you won't be guided by it. The quickest way to gain entry to the mediocre sales club is to choose winging it over planning it.

*A*sk. Six months ago I saw an article in <u>The Competitive</u> <u>Advantage</u> newsletter with the headline - "The Most Powerful Three Letter Word." You guessed it, the word was "ask." In sales the principle tool we use to help customers buy our products are words. Words are our tools. We live and die by them. Sales are won and lost by the proper or improper usage of words. When you ask really good questions, not the shoot from the lip variety, you show interest. There's no easier way to learn more about your prospects. Many salespeople recognize the value of good questions, but fail to properly execute. One of the biggest roadblocks to developing customers and prospects is our own mouth. Instead of spending time "telling," start spending some time "asking."

*V*oice. So, how do you sound? Do you like the way you talk? Is your grammar okay? Is your pacing smooth? Are you making proper use of inflection? What kind of tone beams from your conversational voice? Do you pepper your language with trite useless expressions like "ya know," "okay," and "uh huh?" Do you always smile when speaking on the phone? Most of us want to say we don't have any of these bad habits. There's only one way to be certain. You must periodically record your conversations, especially telephone calls. Thirty minutes of tape being replayed for your personal benefit will really open your eyes, unplug your ears, and help you to connect your mouth to your brain. What you say is anchored to how you say it. Treat yourself to what your customers hear. You'll either love it or hate it. Why risk not knowing.

*E*valuate. There's an old axiom, "What gets measured gets done." Here's an example, borrowed from the game of golf. Each month the top golf magazines publish statistics. Each golfer is ranked on such things as average length of drives, number of putts per round, percentage of greens hit in regulation, percentage of fairways hit with the drive, percentage of sand trap saves, total number of birdies, total number of eagles, average strokes per round, and cumulative earnings. You'd have to agree, if you were a professional golfer, these are the critical measurements of success.

Aren't there critical measurements for salespeople? What are the measures in your business? Recording statistics for close ratios, number of calls to close, average dollars per sale, total sales in key product lines, effective margins, and your income, will help you measure your success. What could it possibly mean if you aren't effectively measuring the critical components? How could you benefit from knowing how you stacked up to the other selling pros? Would this information help you when you're practicing? If you believe that "what gets measured, gets done," you better start measuring. Determine the critical measurements for your business and start your personal statistics log.

The road to change is paved with learning.

Everyone thinks of changing the world, but no one thinks of changing himself.
Tolstoy

Both tears and sweat are salty, but they render a different result. Tears will get you sympathy, sweat will get you change.
Jesse Jackson

#17

You'll Never Get
Orange Juice From Squeezing Lemons

You'll never get orange juice from squeezing lemons, and you'll never achieve superstar status in sales if you don't do the right stuff. The right stuff includes a number of things that most winners focus on.

A written plan. Consistently achieving success isn't about luck. It has more to do with planning. Pilots, ships' captains, and long distance drivers all rely on charts and maps to get where they're going. So do the best of the best salespeople. They realize, "you get what you plan."

Specific dollar goals. Straight commission salespeople will have dollar goals listing sales for specific products with completion dates. Other salespeople may record sales goals by major accounts Recognize and appreciate the benefits of planning instead of settling for what you get.

Mental exercises. This is a high-impact, low-time commitment essential. You can't sell cold turkey every day. Limbering-up and tuning-up are critical for sustaining success. Fifteen minutes a day represents 1% of a day. If you commit to reading periodicals and books on selling for just fifteen minutes daily - you will achieve greater knowledge that automatically converts to competitive advantage. In time your knowledge base grows geometrically as will your results.

Physical exercise. So many people talk about the benefits of regular exercise that there has to be something to it. On a recent flight from Chicago to Orlando, I was seated next to an overweight businessman. When dinner came he literally cleaned his entire tray, and you can bet what his response was when the flight attendant asked if he wanted a big chocolate chip cookie. I guess if we could learn to balance our food with liberal doses of regular exercise, we'd feel, look, and certainly perform a lot better. Imagine your epitaph describing you by the food you ate.

"Yes I can" vs. "Yes I can't" attitude. Not a day goes by that I don't observe negative self-talk. People saying they can't do something even before they begin trying. Think of all the innovation that would have been stifled if the hesitators ruled the world. It's bad enough that they are in the majority. If you would start every day with a sober, expectant, and positive look in the mirror uttering positive cheerleading type words, I know more mountains would be climbed.

Purposeful passion. What is purposeful passion if it isn't a look you have in your eyes. It's the steady focus on pre-set goals that are pursued energetically and enthusiastically every day. The face smiles, the eyes sparkle, and the adrenaline flows. People with purpose walk faster. People with passion have fire in their bellies. When was the last time you got very excited about anything? The only time you should expect not to see purpose and passion is when you're visiting a cemetery. For them it's too late, for us there's no excuse. For us there are only choices.

Always ask, "How can I do it better?" One of the biggest challenges we face as we move closer to the 21st Century is battling complacency. Complacency is like kudzu, that overwhelming weed that's taking over the southeast. Instinctively we want to rely on more of the same. We feel comfortable with what is comfortable. Old habits die hard and new habits are even harder to jump start. Get a rubber stamp made with the words, "How can I do it better?" Stamp everything with it so you never forget that your mission is continuous improvement in everything you do.

Learn to flirt. Your selling skills and techniques should be changing constantly. Small and incremental changes allow you to flirt with new strategies and measure their success rate. Future prosperity will be linked to personal growth and change. Buzz words you should cling to are stretching, adapting, adopting, reinventing and re-engineering. They are the fabric of change.

> **The will to win is not nearly as important as the will to prepare to win.**
>
> **Bobby Knight**

> **Winning is a reflex action. If you've been there in your mind, you'll go there in your body.**
>
> **Denis Waitley**

> **Whoever said, "It's not whether you win or lose that counts," probably lost.**
>
> **Martina Navratilova**

#18

Wanna Double Sales?

It all began when I was returning from a three-day, three-city, sales training trip. My car was parked at the O'Hare garage.

I don't often park at the O'Hare Airport parking garage. I usually opt for a limo to and from the airport, because of some damage to my car a while back. After completing a program in the Chicago area I had to catch a flight to Indianapolis. Driving to the airport made the most sense.

So, at the end of the three day trip, I returned to O'Hare, successfully claimed my luggage and headed for the garage. To get to the garage from the United Airlines terminal, I had to walk through tunnel # 2. As I entered the tunnel, I could faintly hear the familiar sounds of a saxophone player in the distance. The mellow tunes offered a nice welcome home.

Walking down the tunnel, I saw three little boys about ten years old. They were chanting, "Hey mister, wanna buy some candy?" over and over again. I walked right past them.

After about ten steps, I had thoughts of a very successful week and the opportunity to help these kids in a small way. So with luggage in hand I turned around and walked back into their "Hey mister, wanna buy some candy?"

I asked one kid what the deal was. He said, "We're trying to get money for baseball uniforms, wanna buy some candy?" I asked, "How much?" He said, "Two bucks." I bought a yellow bag of M&M peanut candy.

Holding the candy, I turned and headed toward the garage, and once again heard the chorus of "Hey mister, wanna buy some candy?" I spontaneously thought these kids needed some help with their selling skills. Again, I turned around and headed back to the kids.

As soon as I reached them I asked, "How would you like to double sales?" They almost went into shock on the spot. They looked at me with their eyes wide open, nodding their heads and eager to learn how.

Of the three little kids, one seemed to have a natural smile. I pointed to the other two and said "You two - you have to smile. Go ahead and try it." They did as they were instructed. Immediately, their street-tough faces turned warm and child-like.

As I continued my spontaneous sales seminar I said, "In addition to smiling, remember this. Everybody says - 'Hey mister, wanna buy some candy?' To be successful, you have to be different. Try something like this. 'How would you like to help us little guys get baseball uniforms by buying some candy?' I repeated it for them and said, 'That's all you have to do.'"

I turned for the last time and headed for the garage. To my total amazement, I could hear the echo in the tunnel of the three kids, each enthusiastically saying "How would you like to help us little guys get baseball uniforms by buying some candy?" I almost couldn't believe what I was hearing.

When I got home, I told Bernadette, my wife, I had just given the best program I had ever given in my life. I then told her what happened.

Long into the night and the next day, I couldn't help wondering why every program wasn't as good as the one I had given to those three kids.

I guess it's because kids trust, try, and triumph, while adults doubt, delay, and do nothing. Maybe we should be more like kids again.

> **We must change to master change.**
> **Lyndon Johnson**

> **Our dilemma is that we hate change and love it at the same time; what we want is for things to remain the same but get better.**
> **Sydney Harris**

> **To change and change for the better are two different things.**
> **German Proverb**

51

#19

Which Comes First?

A sign in front of a local deli in my neighborhood reads: "Quick! Hire a teenager while he still knows it all." Parents can attest to the fact that most teens do think they know it all. We probably felt the same way when we were teenagers. Yet as we grow older we change our tune from "I know it all" to "I can't wait until I know it all." So, which comes first confidence or competence?

Feeling "that we know it all" let's us feel more confident, and confidence plays a big role in most selling situations. For example, new sales representatives lack confidence in most things and veteran representatives feel their confidence challenged when selling new products to new customers.

Technology also has an impact on our confidence. You may be more accustomed to using slide rules and calculators than to dealing with your newly equipped virtual office that does everything but feed the dog, and you can bet they're working on that.

There aren't many things that can thwart the efforts of a sales rep more than lack of confidence. Once your customer or prospect senses this weakness, you're in a situation that would scare most pit bulls.

Confidence naturally is linked to competence. They aren't

measured in equal amounts. It's never a one-to-one relationship. Yet, when asked, many salespeople will actually admit to trying to hurry their competence, in order for their confidence to catch up.

Fact one - you can't hurry competence. Competence is a function of time.

Fact two - confidence is more related to attitude than to competence.

If you are the surgeon's first patient, the dentist's first root canal, or the new pilot's first passenger, you expect competence; but, you also want to see confidence. As long as we don't wear our competence on badges, we must do everything to boost our confidence.

Confidence screams - what's yours shouting? Remember competence takes time. Confidence just takes the right attitude.

Most of us realize we'll never "know it all." But by trying to "learn it all" we'll be working on our confidence and competence. Think of these two C's - confidence and competence - as the backbone of SUCCESS.

> **We must be trying to learn who we are rather than trying to tell ourselves who we should be.**
>
> **John Powell**

#20

Unspoken Thank You's

How many times during the day, over the course of a week, or over the span of a year is a deserved "thank you" unspoken and, of course, unheard?

"Jim, thanks for a great job." That's all it said, but it was enough. That's what was written on Larry B.'s business card that he put in my sports jacket pocket. Four days earlier, I had given a sales training presentation to Larry's sales force. It was my third annual presentation with his group.

I found the note as I walked from my rental car to the Inn at Eagle Creek, in southern Illinois, where I was scheduled for a keynote presentation.

The note put a smile on my face and reminded me of Larry in a special way. Larry took the time to make my day. How many times a day are we in a position to do what Larry did? My guess is more than we'd care to admit. But how often do we do what Larry did? My guess is less than we'd care to admit.

Recognition is a powerful and persuasive motivator. It doesn't take much to become a master motivator, just some well-placed and well-deserved thank you's. Thank you's are used so sparingly they are becoming an endangered species. Here's my criteria for giving thank you's. Quite simply, give them to anyone who makes your day a little better.

There are endless ways to communicate your appreciation. There is the straight forward verbal approach. You can phone or send a FAX. You can send a hand-written note or even a more formal letter with copies to everybody. There's also voice-mail and E-mail. It doesn't matter how you do it.

For me, I'll take Larry's one-liner on his business card any time. Thank you Larry for making my day.

Human beings, like plants, grow in the soil of acceptance, not in the atmosphere of rejection.

John Powell

We must not only give what we have; we must also give what we are.

Cardinal Mercier

Gratitude is the most exquisite form of courtesy.

Anonymous

Our favorite attitude should be gratitude.

Anonymous

#21

Lessons From The Game Of Golf

In the game of golf, your ability is measured by a calculated handicap. The lower your handicap the better you are.

In my sales training seminars, I often ask for a volunteer. The volunteer has to meet only one criteria. He or she must have an average score in the nineties for eighteen holes of golf. A person shooting in the nineties is considered to be a high handicapper or an average golfer.

I ask the volunteer to step forward and to face the group. Next, I tell the volunteer that I'm going to ask him to take three imaginary golf shots. His instructions are to address the imagined ball and take a swing based on the situation described.

For the first shot, I ask my volunteer to imagine he is on the first tee hitting a driver. I ask him to address the ball and take his normal driver swing. Next I ask him to imagine he's on a long par five and seventy yards from the pin. Once again, I ask him to address the ball and take his regular swing with the wedge. Finally, I'll ask him to imagine he's on the seventh hole only ten yards from the green. Once again, I'll ask him to pick his club, and take his swing.

After three imaginary swings, I'll ask for a round of applause, and ask him to be seated. It never fails - each time I ask a high handicapper to swing a club - he does it with confidence and without hesitation.

After the demonstration, I'll always ask the volunteer if he ever played professional golf or earned a great deal of money playing the game. Always the response is the same, "Of course not."

Let's review what's happened. An average golfer, without hesitation, without a golf club, without a golf ball, and without grass will enthusiastically demonstrate the art of golf in front of all his peers and managers.

Then, I ask for another volunteer. I ask for a person who would be willing to demonstrate, in front of his entire organization, how to make a telephone appointment, approach a prospect, use open ended questions, handle price objections, and finally how to ask for the order.

It's amazing - I've never had any volunteers. Wonder why? It's difficult to demonstrate something you haven't practiced and for which you have no routine.

Even the average golfer, who isn't being paid for what he does, has a backpack of skills. As he approaches each shot, he knows which club he will select, how he will address the ball, and how he will adjust his swing arc and his speed. He has practiced a variety of shots, and has established a routine that gives him confidence.

Even more importantly, as he plays the round, he will engage in a process of self-evaluation and self-analysis. He will decide what worked and what didn't, and make changes as he approaches his next shots. He mentally sees each shot as a way to improve upon a previous shot.

For no particular reason and without any rationale, salespeople are reluctant to prepare and practice the specific words they use in critical situations. Most prefer instead, to act with random spontaneity. It's as though preparation means sounding canned, and of course salespeople never want to sound canned. If you want your words to be crisp, concise, and have the maximum impact on your prospect, never wait until you're with your prospect to prepare what you're going to say.

Treating every call as an adventure is out. What's in, is preparing and practicing, for each critical element of the sales call.

> **Practice does not make perfect; perfect practice makes perfect.**
> **Vince Lombardi**

> **Don't do anything in practice that you wouldn't do in a game.**
> **George Halas**

> **In all things, success depends upon previous preparation, and without such preparation, there is failure.**
> **Confucius**

#22

Check Your Exuders

It's all about attitude isn't it? "What's about attitude?" you're wondering. Selling success is about attitude isn't it? I'm always asking salespeople how they define the word attitude. They usually respond the same way.

When I take all their words and distill it down to a very few, attitude is about what we feel and what we exude. It's about what's inside and what's outside.

I also like to ask the salespeople in my seminars what they want to exude. Here's a sample of how they often reply. "I want to exude . . . confidence, knowledge, competence, sincerity, credibility, trust, reliability, empathy, enthusiasm, excitement, passion, consistency, professionalism, preparation, creativity, and resourcefulness."

I hope you'll agree that wanting to exude and actually exuding may be two entirely different things. Wanting isn't enough and wanting isn't doing. What you exude is critical to how you are perceived. How you are perceived is critical to how well you are liked. How well you are liked is critical to the buyer buying what you are selling.

Ultimately what you feel and what you exude not only get you to first base, they are essential if you want to be in a position to score.

Here are several ideas on how to check your exuders.

1. Always have positive expectations. Expect to win and you will win more of the time.

2. Always use positive self-talk when preparing to see a prospect or customer.

3. Never forget to put your smile to work.

4. Powerful exuders tend to influence others. Check reactions to check your exuders.

5. There's no downtime when it's showtime. When you're in front of a prospect or customer, you'd better be on.

6. Make sure your eyes sparkle. If you can't get excited about your product, please don't think the customer will.

Most folks won't judge you by how much you know as much as they will by how you come across to them. Never make a sales call without checking your exuders. Don't leave home without them.

Remember, whatever game you play, 90% of success is from the shoulders up.
Arnold Palmer's father

#23

Dare To Be Different

On February 25, 1995, I had an assignment with the United States Postal Service in Cooperstown, New York-the home of the Baseball Hall Of Fame. To get there I flew with United Airlines. In most aspects except for one it was a very normal and thankfully safe flight.

My flying partner, that's how flight attendants refer to people who don't know each other and have to sit together, was an elderly gentleman who had flown for more than fifty years.

It was a short flight with a lunch served. On this flight I was fortunate enough to be seated in first class, thanks to an upgrade coupon. I use those coupons every chance I can. It's a nice way to fly, especially if you fly often.

During the flight, I busied myself with preparing for my full day seminar with the northeast region of the U.S. Postal Service. I was really looking forward to working with this group, and I especially was looking forward to catching even a glimpse of what Cooperstown was all about.

Ten minutes before we landed, something happened that I had never experienced before or since. The gentleman next to me hadn't experienced it either in all his years of flying. Judging from the buzz in first class, neither had

any of the other passengers. Just before we landed the
first flight attendant passed out business cards from the
pilot with a handwritten note on the back. Here's what
mine said on the back of the card.

4/24/95

Mr. Meisenheimer -

Thanks for riding to Albany with us today.

We appreciate all your business!

2 -C

Rob Escallon

There are 54,000 employees with United Airlines and 9,000
of them are pilots. How many of them take the time to
handwrite a short note like Captain Rob? In all the years
I've been flying, it's the first one I ever received. The
fellow next to me, who had flown twice as long as I had,
said it was a first for him too. The buzz we heard
throughout first class indicated we were all sharing in a
first-time experience.

That little gesture made many folks grin a little and
appreciate the top notch pilot we had flying the plane.
I've mentioned this during a number of my selling skills
seminars. Just recently, as soon as I finished sharing this
with a group, a Senior VP raised his hand and excitedly

told the group that he too had flown with Captain Rob several years ago, and had also received one of his cards.

All of Captain Rob's passengers remember him; how many of your customers and prospects remember you? When you do something different, you can expect to be remembered.

> Some of us will do our jobs well and some will not, but we will all be judged by only one thing - the result.
>
> Vince Lombardi

> To raise new questions, new possibilities, to regard old problems from a new angle, requires creative imagination.
>
> Albert Einstein

> Ideas are like rabbits. You get a couple and learn how to handle them, and pretty soon you have a dozen.
>
> Anonymous

> Do not let what you cannot do interfere with what you can do.
>
> John Wooden

#24

Are You Still Sounding Pathetic?

Don't say:

What are your needs?

I was in the area . . .

We're the best in the business.

Is price important to you?

Are you the decision-maker?

What do you think?

When will you make a decision?

Have you looked at the information I sent you?

We are very price competitive.

I see your point, but . . .

What time would be good for you?

When can you let me know?

Can I call you in two weeks?

Are you having any problems with . . .

Can I help you?

I don't know.

We can't do that.

Hang on a minute.

It's our company policy to . . .

What do I have to do to earn your business?

Did you get the information I sent?

What do you have for me today?

So, what do you think?

I need you to . . .

You'll have to . . .

I was wondering . . .

I think maybe I can . . .

How soon do you need it?

I'm not sure if . . .

Did you get a chance to look at the proposal?

What's going on?

Can I be honest?

In my own mind . . .

The words you use, create the image you leave behind.

**Every man takes the limits of his own
field of vision for the limits of the world.**
                              Schopenhauer

**People are great manufacturers. Some
make good, others make trouble, and
some just make excuses.**
                              Anonymous

#25

It All Adds Up

How important is financial security? If you believe it's very important, as most of us do, another question must be asked: How will you achieve it? For salespeople, it can be an especially vexing problem, since incomes can vary so much from year to year.

There are many things that frustrate regular savings plans. When you're young, single, and starting out, you probably have your eyes on a condo or town house. Marriage and family add new dimensions. First there's the house and then there are kids, which begin a real drain on savings. A survey conducted by the Rand Corporation revealed that 50% percent of the people in the U.S. between the ages fifty-one and sixty had an average net worth of less than $100,000, including home equity. Only 5% of the same age group had a net worth exceeding $850,000.

When it comes to financial security, how do you define yours? Depending on your age, if you haven't started to think about it, it may already be too late. Here are several things to keep in mind. It's all about net worth; not about the things you possess. It's all about the difference between what you own and what you owe - net worth. Net worth provides leverage and yields genuine security and peace of mind.

The rule of seventy-two is every investor's best friend. The rule states that you can determine how long it will take your investment to double simply by dividing seventy-two by either the interest rate or growth rate. For example, if you invest $2,500 with a return of 6% annually, your money will double in twelve years. Another thing to remember and it's critical to success, is that starting to save is always tougher than continuing to save. The savings habit is hard to kill once it's born.

I've saved the best for last. When you save regularly and start young, you're in the best position to benefit from compounding. I wish someone would have explained compounding to me when I was a teenager.

It all adds up. When you start young, save regularly, and benefit from the effects from compounding you'll end up with a bucket full of net worth. To get a jump start, you need to be street smart and head smart.

While smart investing habits won't help you sell, it will add dramatically and perhaps geometrically to the rewards of skillful selling. A true professional will build a savings program into his earnings.

> **Friendship is like money - easier made than kept.**
> **Anonymous**

> **Taking your money with you when you die isn't important. The real problem is making it last until you're ready to go.**
> **Anonymous**

#26

Savvy Time Tips

Successful salespeople always have priorities and they diligently work on them. They relentlessly strive not to waste their time. They are especially good at keeping lists and really good at prioritizing items on their lists.

To use your time wisely, remember these action points.

- ■ Plan everything.
- ■ Prioritize everything.
- ■ Do everything that's important.
- ■ Do everything that's important first.
- ■ Remember fifteen minutes is 1% of a day.
- ■ Doing is more important than thinking.
- ■ Finished is better than perfect.
- ■ Time is finite. When it's gone it's gone.

To keep yourself on track, periodically ask yourself the following questions:

Am I making the best use of my time right now?

Should I be working on something more important?

Do I feel in control of my time and my life?

Do I spend more time regretting things I've done or things I haven't done?

Have I taken the time to write on paper my life goals?

Do I have completion dates for all the priorities I have, especially closing big prospects?

What is my time perspective . . . past, present or future?

Can I succinctly describe the ten things that worry me the most?

If I knew I was going to die within six months, how important would each of the ten things on my list be?

What do I want inscribed on my tombstone?

Am I living my life so that the engraver won't be lying?

When it comes to paperwork, do I handle it only once?

When reading magazines and books, do I only read the articles and chapters that interest me?

Do I start with an outline before writing letters?

Do I use waiting time as a gift of time?

Can I say "no" without feeling guilty?

Remember this about time. "No one has enough time, yet everyone has all there is."

#27

E-Mail Babble

When you communicate, you exchange thoughts, words, and ideas. When you talk on the Internet, especially when using e-mail, techno-babble takes on a whole new dimension.

For example do you recognize these emotions:

‹G ›	=	Grinning
‹L ›	=	Laughing
;-	=	Licking lips
:-J	=	Tongue in cheek
OMG	=	Oh my God!
:X	=	Oops
SGAL	=	Sheesh, get a life
PITA	=	Pain in the ass
IMO	=	In my opinion
****	=	Kisses
BRB	=	Be right back
C U L8R	=	See you later
WDYGU	=	Why don't you grow up
WYSIWYG	=	What you see is what you get
IOH	=	I'm out of here
GG	=	Gotta go

#28

Is Anybody There?

Has this ever happened to you? You're trying to call someone and you dial. After three rings, you hear a very soft click, followed by a message like this.

> Hello, this is (insert name). I'm in the office today, but either on the telephone or temporarily away from my desk. Please leave your name, telephone number, and a brief message after the beep and I'll call you back as soon as I can.

The problem is you rarely get the return call. Did you ever wonder where all the people who never answer their phones hang out? If you're lucky enough to reach a live person, like a secretary, and she tells you the person you're trying to reach is on the telephone, and asks if you want to hold, can you remember the last time you said "yes?" I can't, because it seems when you reach someone on the phone, he usually stays on longer than I'm ever willing to wait.

Here are several creative and practical tips from "How to leave messages that get results" that appeared in <u>The Telephone Selling Report</u>, published by Art Sobczak (800-326-7721).

1. Don't sell your products/services on the message. Ignoring this point is what gets messages thrown away. You don't want to say, "We sell office supplies and I'd like to discuss the possibilities with you."

2. Mention the benefits and results they could potentially get. You could call this a teaser. This is what's going to cause them to listen to the message, stroke their chin and think, "Hmmmm, this is interesting. There might be something here we could use." Which is exactly the reaction you want.

3. Make delivery of the benefits/results contingent on speaking with you. This means that in order for them to find out what you're talking about, they need to speak with you. Use language and tone that conveys the importance of a personal conversation such as, "to determine how our product would be of value to you, we'll need to talk."

4. Let them know who's to do what next. If you're going to call them, be certain to specify a date and time (get this time from the screener.) If they are to call you, (which isn't a good idea on prospecting calls) give a range of times when you'll be available.

Here's an excellent sample message that Art has successfully used:

> I'm Jay Wilson with Tempo Services. We specialize in helping accountants generate more corporate work during non-tax seasons. I'd like to discuss the type of business you'd like to get more of, to see if it would make sense to speak further. I'll try back Tuesday morning before 10:00 AM.

You need to be prepared to leave a message every time you call a prospect or customer. Every contact is an opportunity. With a little preparation and lots of practice you can put the prospect in a frame of mind where he eagerly looks forward to your next call.

Without a prepared message you run the risk of miscommunicating in the style of Casey Stengel and others who got mugged by their own mouths. Stengel became so famous for his confusing messages that his use of the language became known as "Stengelese."

> **Now all you fellows line up alphabetically by height.**
> **Casey Stengel**

> **A lot of people my age are dead at the present time.**
> **Casey Stengel**

> **Half this game is ninety percent mental.**
> **Danny Ozark, manager of the Philadelphia Phillies**

> **We offer the party as a big tent. How we do that within the platform, the preamble to the platform, or what not, that remains to be seen. But that message will have to be articulated with great clarity.**
> **Vice-President Dan Quayle**

#29

Story-Boarding Your Questions

Before you tell your story, get the prospects or customers to tell theirs. Easy to say and hard to do. When you ask questions, especially with new prospects, what specifically are you trying to learn? Imagine the boxes below are three by five cards. Label them with the pieces of information you want to obtain. Also consider the sequence of the questions.

If the purpose of questions, is to uncover needs and to identify the prospect's critical challenges, aren't you really trying to encourage them to tells their story? If you agree, doesn't it also make sense that you should encourage them to tell it in a way that's logical and conversational?

Here's how I approach new prospects in an attempt to get to know them and to identify their specific challenges and needs. See if this works for you.

Situation	Key Players	Responsibility
Challenges	Priorities	Relationship
Suppliers	Products	Decision Criteria
Decision Process	Success Measurement	Getting Started

#30

Tough Customers As Teddy Bears

"I would like a table," I repeated stonily. "I
am a full member of this club." We locked
eyes for a moment. Then he shrugged.
Every eye in the room was on me as he
escorted me to a table. Sometimes, what
starts with a bang, ends with a whimper.

You're probably imagining this exchange taking place at a
country club. Well, it didn't. Actually, the excerpt
appeared in the <u>Chicago Tribune</u> and was describing the
experiences of Laurie Frank, one of 250 women entering
Yale University back in 1969. The above experience
occurred after graduation, in New York City, when she
asked to be served lunch. As a Yale graduate she was
entitled to membership in the Yale Club. There was a
hitch however. Certain privileges of the Yale Club, such as
access to the Grill Room and the pool continued to be
reserved for men only. The rest as you can see is history.

Twenty years ago, as a new sales rep for the Scientific
Products division of American Hospital Supply
Corporation, I tried to get an appointment with John O.,
who was then the administrator for the American Health
Foundation. No matter what I said nor how I said it
proved successful. I was told he was just too busy to see
me. I was a wreck just thinking about my dilemma.

You see, we sold laboratory supplies, and the American Health Foundation was building new laboratories. Back then, life was different and in many ways easier. While I couldn't get in to see the administrator, I did gain access to several directors of the individual labs. I remember one of them placing a rather substantial order with me.

After the order was shipped, I paid a visit to the lab to make sure the lab director was completely satisfied with the entire order and the way it was delivered. The chief administrator's office was located in this wing and as I walked past his office, I saw my chance and waved. He waved back, and not knowing who I was also gestured me in. I finally had my meeting and also discovered why he was impossible to see. Once I got in, I couldn't get out. He loved to talk about the industry. He loved to talk about mutual acquaintances - he loved to talk about everything. It taught me a valuable lesson about some people who say they are too busy to see you. They may not be too busy, they may actually be easily distracted. After our initial meeting, I always managed to see John as often as I liked and I did it without having to make appointments. When there wasn't anyone in his office, I'd stand outside and wave. He would always wave back and wave me in. Over time, John became my second biggest customer.

Remember, don't give up on the ones who say they are too busy. Get creative and you may be setting up the biggest sale you ever made. If it can happen to me, it can happen to you.

Sometimes what starts with a bang, ends with a whimper. Some of the toughest customers I ever had were really teddy bears in disguise.

#31

Making A Difference

It's not often that I have the opportunity to speak to my clients within several weeks of a sales training program. Last September I had such an opportunity. Dan, the sales training manager for a midwest manufacturing company, called to order some books and audio tapes to be used as a follow-up to a training program I did for his company.

During our conversation, he told me about a recent success one of their reps had shared with him. It seems that Jason had been trying unsuccessfully to get an appointment with a big prospect named Hewlett-Packard.

One of the subjects discussed during the sales training session was goal setting. When I presented the topic, I shared three imperatives for proper and effective goal setting. The first and most important rule is that to transform a dream into a goal, it must be committed to writing. Over 95% of all the salespeople I have worked with do not have their personal goals and professional goals in writing.

The second imperative is that effective goals must be specific and measurable. It's amazing how many people consider their goals only in general terms. A goal without specificity is like a target without a bull's-eye, both are useless.

The third imperative is that a goal once defined must have a completion date. Every completion date should have three components. A day, a month, and a year. A set completion date is the fuel that makes the engine run.

Dan mentioned that Jason had just confirmed his appointment with Hewlett-Packard. Jason had been trying unsuccessfully for several months to secure the appointment. After the training program, he wrote down a specific goal. His goal was to get the appointment within thirty days. The result was that he did. His comment to Dan was that writing it down really made a difference.

■ Goals really do make a difference.

■ Very few people make goal setting a priority.

■ Goals are the essential seeds for personal growth.

■ People with goals get extraordinary results.

I was recently asked this question at a seminar. "How many times will I have to hear about goal setting before I do something about it?" The question was much better than my answer, because I didn't know. Some people think and some people act.

Are you a player or a spectator? Your answer depends on what you do, not what you are thinking about doing.

#32

The Price Is Right

You're a salesperson. You sell products. It doesn't matter what kind. Your company gives you some flexibility when it comes to price. Your price has elasticity. You have control.

Question: Which do you think of first, the most you can sell your product for or the least you can sell it for? Be honest!

When asked to justify your answer, do you feel yourself becoming defensive? We are defensive about our opinions, our beliefs, and our values. Most of us are extremely comfortable justifying our positions. Tom Winninger, in his book <u>Price Wars,</u> offers us a choice. He says "We can explain our value or defend our price." Most of us spend our time defending our price. I know I do.

As a professional sales trainer it's not easy for me to admit. I am just as gun-shy about price as you might be. Let me give you a real-life example.

I recently had a phone call from the president of a small, medical supply company. He told me he had five salespeople and an inside customer service person. He was very interested in providing sales training for this small team of his. Two months earlier I had just raised my fees 20%.

The first thought I had after he told me about the size of his organization, was that there was no way I could charge him my new fee. I took my new fee and entered it into my desktop calculator and proceeded to divide it by the number of sales reps he had. It was almost comical as I caught myself talking myself out of a profitable sale.

Well, I couldn't control having that thought, but I could control how I reacted to it. So I began asking open ended questions. I asked him to describe his sales organization. He did in considerable detail. I asked him about previous sales training, and he mentioned there hadn't been any previous training. He reminded me that we had talked three years earlier when he was a sales manager and worked for his father. His father was retired; he was now the President.

I then asked him what made him decide to call me back after three years. He told me about his company's success and his desire to keep the momentum going. Everything about his business was changing - markets, customers, products, competition, and of course the federal government's involvement or meddling with health care. Given all the changes, he viewed sales training not as an option but as a necessity.

A funny thing happened while I was listening to his responses to my questions. He convinced me, yes - he convinced me, to present my new and higher fee. I really wanted to thank him. He'll never know how close I came to giving him a whopping discount two minutes into the telephone call.

That's the story and here's the point. Actually there are two points. First, never give into your negative thoughts especially when they relate to price. Second, never offer a price until you have completed a comprehensive assessment of your prospect's needs. By not jumping the gun, I avoided giving a discount that wasn't necessary.

Get them to tell you their story before you tell yours. And remember, never give a price before you get their story. The price is right when your product matches their needs and when your value exceeds their expectations.

> Good salesmen, like good cooks, create an appetite when the buyer doesn't seem to be hungry.
>
> **Anonymous**

> The price is high. I don't think there's any question about the price being high, Mr. Prospect, but when you add the benefits of quality, subtract the disappointments of cheapness, multiply the pleasure of buying something good, and divide the cost over a period of time, the arithmetic comes out in your favor .... If it costs you a hundred dollars but does you a thousand dollars worth of good, then by any yardstick you've bought a bargain, haven't you?
>
> **Zig Ziglar**

#33

Noteworthy

In a recent sales training seminar for a wholesale drug company, I was sharing ideas on how to become a better listener.

Since I am originally from New York I often tell people how I grew up being a poor listener because I was accustomed to doing everything fast. New Yorkers talk, walk, eat, and drive fast. We also listen fast; and, for me, listening fast has always meant listening poorly.

I told the sales group that there are two ways to improve their listening skills. First, ask rock-solid and oyster-opening questions. Whenever you ask a really good question, you're more likely to get a really good response. The better the response, the more you'll discover about your customer or prospect.

The second thing you must do to become a more effective listener is to take notes. Nothing improves listening more than taking notes.

When you ask questions and take notes you become more focused and more effective. When your ears are working overtime, your mouth has time for a much needed break. The highest compliment seminar participants can give me throughout the program is to take notes. With their note taking, they're communicating by their actions that there is real value in what I'm saying. Note taking makes you noteworthy.

Whenever you'd like to make your customers feel noteworthy, just take some notes. It'll do wonders for their egos and in the process you will gain valuable insight about the customers and their ideas. With the notes you've taken, you create the added benefit of a permanent record.

It's worth taking notes, because you'll make the person you're speaking with feel special and noteworthy.

> If you listen to their words, they will buy from you.
> Jim Meisenheimer

> Big people monopolize the listening. Small people monopolize the talking.
> David Schwartz

> Filling our ears with all we have learned to say, we are deaf to what we have yet to hear.
> Wendell Johnson

> You ain't learnin' nothin' when you're doin' all the talkin'.
> Lyndon Johnson

#34

How To Look Like
You Know What You're Talking About

The way to look like you know what you're talking about is not to talk a lot. That might be easier than it sounds, given the talkativeness of most salespeople. So, if you're not talking, what should you be doing? Here are eleven things to consider:

1. Prepare in advance. If it's prepared, it's more likely to sound professional.

2. Practice power phrases. Turn off the car radio once in a while. Listening to Rush Limbaugh will never put commissions into your pocket. Practicing what you'll say on the next call will.

3. Tell stories (short ones.) Share stories about how other customers are successfully benefiting from using your products.

4. Ask oyster-opening questions. Don't wing the questions or you'll end up sounding like a duck.

5. Take notes. Nothing telegraphs interest and intelligence more than good note taking.

6. Have direct eye contact. The eyes are the windows to the mind. Be sure to use them correctly.

7. Use interjections. When you occasionally use interjections like "I see" and "I understand" it'll help keep the conversation going the right way - with the customer doing more of the talking.

8. Show your products. Be sure to show and emphasize your sales literature, especially photographs.

9. Touch your products. If you're selling tangibles, hold your product as you talk about it. Giving your prospect the product is even better.

10. Be poised. Show poise and limit the noise (too much talking). Learn about poise, what it is and what it isn't.

11. Be yourself. Be genuine and natural. Consider how people react to you. How do you want them to react. Check your exuders. You may not be exuding want you think you are.

Sounding like you know what you're talking about has less to do with talking, and more to do with how *you* present yourself. Sit back, practice good posture, exude confidence and let the customer see a "professional picture." Aggressively leaning forward, invading personal space, and chomping at the bit to give your "sales pitch" only creates a negative image.

Your actions always speak louder than your words.

#35

The Four Most Important Words

According to Ray Pelletier, the leading attitude coach, the four most important words you can use are, "I need your help." Every time you use them, you give someone an opportunity to come to the rescue. These are powerful words and they deliver huge benefits to the people who rely on them to build relationships.

There are three likely scenarios in which to consider using this powerful phrase. First, you can use them when you are a disappointed or disillusioned customer. Second, you may also want to consider using them when interacting with your family. And finally, as a professional sales representative, there are times when these words can really help you.

Airline customers who travel often, will inevitably encounter delays and disappointments. There is another group of words, five to be specific, that make travellers cringe: "Your flight has been cancelled." Ever hear those words before? Of course you have. Imagine an entire boarding area hearing those words. As soon as the words are spoken, there is a scramble to the nearest passenger service representative.

With rage in their hearts, anger on their faces, and pepper in their language, passengers will demand service. I know, I've done it more than I care to admit. Ray's suggestion doesn't "demand," it "requests." It doesn't scream it whispers, "I need your help." When "I need your help" is followed by, "I know it wasn't your fault," strange, unusual and wonderful things begin to happen. You get attention. Your get respect. You also have a better chance of getting the help you need.

As a professional salesperson, you may often experience unforeseen and unexpected changes to your family plans because of job related priorities. Many of us communicate these last minute changes to our spouses or families with words that sound more like excuses than reasons like "I have to do this" "I have to go . . . ." The next time your business interferes with family plans, try saying, "I need your help" to explain the situation. By explaining the situation and asking for help you're more likely to creatively and successfully resolve the situation.

Perhaps the biggest benefit of all goes to the professional sales reps who use these power words when communicating with their customers. A new sales rep meeting customers and prospects for the first time, can gain a significant advantage in most situations simply by saying to the customer, "I need your help." Most customers are willing to help a new sales rep.

You could be a veteran sales rep working with a new product. In this case, asking for the customer's assistance can pay big dividends. You have an opportunity to make the customer feel important to the roll-out or the development of your new products by getting them involved. And it starts by saying, "I need your help."

Another time when you may want to use these words, is when you, your product, or your company lets your customer down. When you ask for their help, you're really asking them for permission to try again.

People are good. Most people derive personal benefit from helping another human being. If you want to make someone feel good and give someone an opportunity to come to your rescue, simply say, "I need your help."

> When you help the fellow who's in trouble, he'll never forget you when you need help.
>
> Anonymous

> The enemy you make today may be the only one who can help you twenty-five years from now.
>
> Anonymous

> Friends in your life are like pillars on your porch. Sometimes they hold you up, and sometimes they lean on you. Sometimes it's just enough to know they're standing by.
>
> Anonymous

> It can be no dishonor to learn from others when they speak good sense.
>
> Sophocles

#36

How To Avoid Becoming
An Incredible Bulk

In his article, "Thin & Now," author Terence Monmaney writes:

> Why do so few men fit into the britches they wore when they set out to conquer the world? Why do we stow the 10 or 20 pounds that usually start trying to sneak aboard in our 30s? A sampling of scientific and medical opinion has turned up a few answers to this innocent question. Yes, it happens to almost everyone. No, it is not an inevitable aging process, like the graying of hair or the paying of tuition. The way some experts see it, you can embark on a state-of-the-art program to help avoid or reduce middle age spread right this second if you get out of your seat and read this standing up.

It's metabolism and it changes with age. Since I just turned fifty, I guess that makes me an expert. Here are some basic facts from Monmaney's researched article.

> First, get moving. Second, stay moving. Physical activity is the key to boosting metabolism, and according to researchers it

does so by creating muscle and reducing
fat. Muscle cells burn far more energy than
fat cells: thus, the higher your ratio of
muscle to fat, the more energy you burn,
and the less fat you accumulate.

I have my own theory. It's about thinking and doing.
When we're younger, we are doing more. Some of us do
considerably more doing before we do any thinking. It's
like we don't care where we are going as long as we're
moving in some direction. Think of it this way. Divide
your age by two. Are most of your regrets in the first half
or second half of your life? Chances are, the older you are
the more regrets you'll have in the first half of your life.
That's because there's a lot of doing without thinking.
Early in life we're burning up more energy because of our
more cooperative metabolism and a higher level of
activity.

As we get older, we take fewer chances. We think before
we do. In extreme cases, mental castration occurs when
we commit ourselves to thinking and procrastinating. In
case you missed the point, thinking doesn't consume any
energy.

So, what can we do to feel and look better. You may want
to check with your doctor before taking any action, but the
odds are that you'll just "think" about it any way.

How to do more to feel better:

1.   Weigh yourself every day. It's really hard to put on
     a lot of pounds this way. You see them one at a
     time.

2. Forget fad diets and exercise programs. They don't yield long-term effects.

3. Do lots of daily stuff. Take vitamins daily. Exercise daily.

4. Listen to music when you exercise - you'll extend your work out session.

5. Give up one soft drink a week. The cumulative effect is 7,500 calories a year.

6. Walk to the store, mail box or any place where the exercise outweighs the distance.

7. Use the stairs instead of the elevator.

8. Bring some exercise gear when you're travelling Engage in running, lifting light-weights, playing tennis or swimming.

9. Avoid the deadly combination of late-night dinners and recliners.

10. Skip all dinner rolls. Guess how many calories that adds up to in a year. Do the math to calculate this biggie. Do you know what percentage of your spare tire comes from bread? Ouch!

Remember, very few people die because they are in shape. Being fit is a state of mind. It's been a great experience for me to write this chapter, because it's reminded me of what I'm reminding you to do.

If you think of any other ways to become more active so I can boost my metabolism, please send an E-mail to: JMCSP@aol.com.

#37

Quote Taker

How's your sales pitch? Do you believe it's really good? It may not be as good as you think it is. A pitch is something that is delivered over and over again. It doesn't change from one customer to the next. That's why it's called a pitch. Professional salespeople don't pitch, they present tailored solutions to very specific customer problems.

The best way to identify customer problems is to ask questions. The preferred questions are open-ended. They get people to open up about specific topics.

You can dramatically increase your probability for success whenever you can identify specific and unique customer requirements. Customers and prospects use words to describe their problems. Ideally, whenever we can relate our product or service to the customer's specific needs the solution will be more appealing to the customer.

Just like customers who use words to relate problems and needs, salespeople also use words to present solutions in the form of products and services. The common denominator is words, the essence of verbal communications. A sales pitch generally uses the same words over and over. A tailored presentation will rely on more appropriate words to present customer-specific solutions. Let me illustrate the point.

When I'm the customer I define service as "on time, every time, and you fix it if it's broken." What if you asked a customer about his priorities and he replied service was a top priority. If you go no further, how will you define service? You would use your own words which may or not match the customer's definition.

Suppose you asked the customer to define service for you. He replies, "Service is what I want, when I want it and how I want it delivered." When you begin to describe the service element for your product, how will you do it? A rep relying on a standard pitch will utter some old and worn comment about service.

The professional sales representative will use a third alternative. He was listening. He was even taking notes. He captured the customer's definition of service as soon as he said it. He even put it in quotes. He captured the important words used by the customer. He wants to relate to the customer, and he knows he has a better chance to connect if he relates to the customer's definition of service by using the customer's key words.

Taking notes is great and a necessity. Taking quotes is even better, and will significantly raise the bar in your attempt to connect with your customer.

Make quote-taking a part of your note-taking.

Remember, if you listen to their words, they will buy from you.

#38

Dealing With Voice-Mail

It used to be, the toughest challenges occurred when you were face-to-face with your prospect or customer. Today, with the advent of universal voice-mail systems, the primary challenge is getting face-to-face with that same prospect or customer.

Voice-mail, when used improperly can reek havoc among sales professionals. Voice-mail was designed to facilitate communications. In reality, salespeople often use it to hide from their sales managers; prospects and customers use it to avoid salespeople; and almost everyone has learned to adapt the written memo to verbal communication resulting in overloaded telephone mail boxes. The communications buck stops with you. Here are a few ideas:

1. Don't use voice mail like memos. Forget about trying to look good by voice copying the world on your activities. Remember this imperative, less is really more.

2. Tired refrains when leaving messages just don't work. Boring - "please return my call," won't create callbacks from busy prospects and customers.

3. Creativity makes the difference. Sounding different gets results. Try using humor, especially when calling

someone who has a reputation for not returning calls. "Bill, I'm so desperate, that I'm considering giving up golf until I hear from you." Before you scoff at the idea, remember, your present approach may not be getting the return call.

4. Funny FAX's also work. Try keeping a cartoon/comic file. The next time you're having trouble getting a return phone call, consider sending a funny FAX. This is another good reason why you should always get the FAX number for your prospects and customers.

5. Punch "O." Most voice mail systems allow you to connect to a real person by dialing "O" almost any time during the message. If after several frustrating attempts of not getting through, seek out a secretary or an assistant. See if they have access to your contact's calendar. If they do, ask them to pencil in a telephone appointment that's mutually convenient.

Dealing with voice-mail is here to stay. Personal creativity and resourcefulness may help your success rate in getting call-backs.

Remember, if you want to make a difference, you have to be different.

I'll pay more for a man's ability to express himself than for any other quality he might possess.
Charles Schwab

#39

Stand-Up Presentations That Stand Out

The next time you're preparing to give a stand up or group presentation, remember there are only three essential things to consider. How will you prepare before the presentation? What will you do during the presentation? What can you do after every presentation to make the next one even better? The key to delivering professional presentations rests in what you do before, during and after each one.

First, be aware of the three B's. Use them and you'll do well. Abuse them and you won't.

- Be yourself
- Be natural
- Be alive

Second, you should be aware of the five biggest mistakes presenters make.

- Not being yourself
- Forgetting simplicity
- Reading your writing
- Being unprepared
- Ignoring visuals

As long as presenters present, these mistakes will be made. If you want to stand out as a stand-up speaker avoid these five mistakes like the plague and you'll do great.

Here are some additional tips, hints, and other practical ideas you can use to prepare for high impact presentations.

1. Less is always more.
2. Focus on what you want them to remember.
3. Avoid too many details.
4. Don't fall in love with your technology.
5. Beware of the dreaded monotone.
6. Remember attention spans are getting shorter.
7. Do something that says you're real.
8. Use performance cues.
9. Remember to create periodic power pauses.
10. It's okay to be imperfect.
11. Have some fun.
12. Make it easy to remember - three R's, four B's.
13. Be passionate.
14. Create strategic landscapes.
15. Make your approach, "There you are" vs. "Here I am."
16. Don't cling to anything.
17. Make it a conversation instead of a presentation.

Anybody can get up in front of a group and talk. It takes lots of preparation and some practice to give a professional presentation. If you really care about your prospect or customer, you won't dare wing your next presentation. The next time you stand-up be sure you stand-out.

> **Some speeches are like broiled lobster. You have to pick through an awful lot to find any meat.**
>
> **Anonymous**

> **The recipe for a good speech includes quite a bit of shortening.**
>
> **Anonymous**

> **A speech is like a love affair - any fool can start one, but it requires considerable skill to end one.**
>
> **Anonymous**

> **To communicate, put your thoughts in order; give them a purpose; use them to persuade, to instruct, to discover, to seduce.**
>
> **William Safire**

> **It usually takes me more than three weeks to prepare a good impromptu speech.**
>
> **Mark Twain**

#40

How Many Plugs
Do You Have In Your Office?

If you want to really unleash your personal and professional potential, you must be able to harness new technology. I realize that any list of new technology quickly becomes out-dated. The following is a list of things that are connected to plugs that have added significantly to my personal and professional productivity.

- Computer
- Monitor (color)
- Notebook computer
- Reusable disk drive (extra storage)
- Modem/FAX
- FAX
- Laser printer
- Color printer
- GBC electronic binding machine
- Stereo player and recorder
- Video recorder
- Verifone - for accepting Visa and Mastercard
- Execufold - for letter folding
- Copier

- Electronic weighing balance
- Postage meter
- Telephone (separate FAX line)
- Telephone headset
- Personal color scanner
- High intensity desk lamps
- Ameritech voice mail system
- Car phone
- Scan Partner Jr.

Technology allows you to transform opportunity into business quickly and effortlessly. Don't be afraid of technology. Make it your partner. Learn to change as it changes and you'll never get bumped off the express lane on the information super highway.

Well, well - the world must turn upon its axis;
And all mankind turn with it, heads or tails
And live and die, make love and pay our taxes,
And, as the veering wind shifts, shift our sails.
George Gordon Byron

Change is the law of life. And those who look only to the past or present are certain to miss the future.

John Fitzgerald Kennedy

#41

The Golden Question

There is indeed a golden question. It's the one question that creates a literal fortune for all who ask it. It doesn't really matter what your profession is, though it works particularly well for salespeople.

This question is difficult to ask because it requires us to search within ourselves. Our best questions are usually reserved for others. We generally prefer to ask questions not answer them.

What's odd about the times we live in, is that as we rapidly approach the 21st Century, everything around us is steeped in rapid change. The world is changing faster than we can keep up. How are we to survive in an environment if we aren't changing as fast as it is? Surviving is only the beginning. How are we to prosper in that same environment if constant change isn't a part of our daily diet? The answer has more to do with the question than with your answer.

If change were so easy everyone would be doing it handily. The fact is that change, especially personal change, isn't easy. Just because it isn't easy doesn't mean we can ignore it. Little changes are tough. Big changes are tougher. Radical changes are toughest.

My advice on changing is simple. Don't plan on making big changes to keep up with your changing environment. Instead, consistently make lots of little changes. If you're always making little changes, after a while the impact becomes big. The significance of lots of little changes is big results.

Here's the golden question: "How can I do it better?" If you ask this question about all aspects of your work, one thing is inevitable you will make lots of changes. When you change, you grow. When you grow you prosper.

As a professional salesperson imagine asking this question about each of the key elements of selling.

How can I do it better?

- Prospecting
- Making appointments
- Building rapport
- Assessing customer needs
- Asking questions
- Making presentations
- Handling concerns
- Negotiating
- Communicating skills
- Securing commitment
- Automating sales
- Writing proposals
- Profiling your customers
- Writing skills

- Communicating non-verbally
- Managing time
- Managing the boss
- Working with peers
- Knowing my products
- Leaving voice mail messages
- Leaving E-mail messages
- Managing my territory
- Managing my accounts
- Managing myself
- Managing the sales call
- Managing the selling cycle
- Managing the sales funnel
- Mastering technology

Make a 1% improvement in each of the above areas by asking the golden question.

> **People who want to stay in business should learn how to cope with change.**
> **Barbara Morgenstern**

> **Markets change, tastes change, so the companies and individuals who choose to compete in those markets must change.**
> **Dr. An Wang**

#42

To Change Or Not To Change?

To change or not to change? That's the real question. It has little to do with being nobler or wiser, and everything to do with advancing and moving into the 21st Century.

We are surrounded with change and yet we hesitate to climb aboard. Why is that? If change is so constant why do we often wait for the last minute to embrace it? Frequently I conduct three or four day seminars. With only rare exceptions, participants will claim the same table and same seat on day two. It takes less than a day for us to completely stake out our territory.

While change isn't easy, it is necessary. Here are some ideas salespeople must consider changing in order to grow their businesses.

Communications - All the rules are changing. Traditional forms of communicating i.e., letters and memos may becoming extinct. The computer is quickly becoming the centerpiece for important communications. The Internet has created a virtual hybrid mall allowing users to do what was unthinkable just several years ago.

You don't need a FAX machine to send or receive FAX'S. With the onset of PC video conferencing you may not need a car to call on customers as often as you think.

Learn to at least flirt with technology if you haven't already fallen in love with it. There is no way to be successful in sales without using a computer.

Humor - Lighten up for Pete's sake. Most folks take things too seriously. I should know, since I count myself as one of the serious brigade. Corporations reek havoc on employees. Managers overwork subordinates. Spouses don't take time to listen to each other. Kids don't see their parents laugh enough. Humor isn't necessarily derived from jokes. It's the stuff the funny bone is made of. A smile when connected to a laugh works miracles. When it comes to day to day stuff, try putting a new spin on it. I recommend at least one good belly laugh a day.

Altitude - Is your reach beyond your grasp? If yes, that's good. If it's not, expand your thinking and reset your goals. When it comes to goals do you think about incremental or quantum gains? Your altitude is keenly influenced by your attitude and the goals you've personally set for yourself. With reality as your barometer, set goals that stretch you to the limit of your capabilities. Don't accept limits set by others.

Niche - You can't be all things to all people. You can't be all places all the time. You can't treat all customers alike. To niche is to focus. It's easy to work hard, it's better to work smart. Discover the art of wide niching and narrow selling. Remember, your focus doesn't have to myopic. You can effectively niche your products, your markets, your customers and your time.

Growth - This is a really big one. There's personal growth, professional growth, territory growth, account growth and that's just the tip of the iceberg. When you measure personal development, what is your yardstick? It should be putting into practice the ideas and strategies you've garnered by the courses and seminars you've attended, the magazines you've read, the books you've purchased and read, and the audio cassette tapes you listen to over and over again. Growing is about not being satisfied with the familiar and routine. Growers are always chipping away at their environment.

There are several significant signs of growth. When you're in a growth mode, you seldom feel comfortable. Growth implies stretching and reaching. Growth also means risk and risk also means occasional set backs. When you're growing you're changing everything, sometimes 1% at a time. If you're not changing, you're stagnant. Stagnant salespeople seldom win new customers.

Excitement - First loves, first jobs, first experiences of any type, generally get people excited. Why is it so many people look sullen instead of excited. Excited people really make a difference. They are the people we want to be around. Last week Bill was cutting my hair, he owns a very unique and old fashioned barber shop in Mundelein, Illinois. We began talking about a mutual friend who was in town. Bill said, "Every time John comes into the shop, I become energized. He's got so much energy and excitement, some of it always rubs off on me."

Excitement is in the eyes. Do yours sparkle? Excitement exudes from your words and your body language. Excitement is what your face says when you're not talking.

To change or not to change? That is the question, and the choice is up to you.

#43

Basic Instincts

Let's review our basic instincts. Oh, not those. That was good, this is better. I'm referring to the basic instincts of professional salespeople, especially the ones that guide us through our daily challenges of selling. You see, these instincts are so basic they may actually create problems that could be avoided.

Be wary of basic instincts.

Talking vs. listening. This is a big one. All business surveys indicate salespeople talk too much. It's because we're great communicators. We often get hired because of our communication skills. When our minds become full of product information, we feel the need to vent. Usually it's right in front of a prospect or customer. Talking is easy, listening is not, especially for good communicators. Remember, if you listen to their words, they will buy from you.

Defending vs. explaining. This is both common and obvious. When you expect your customers to bring up price, you are naturally ready to discuss it. We usually become so preoccupied with pricing matters, it often takes away from really developing the relevant value of the product and how it is tailored to the customer's needs. Tom Winninger, in his book <u>Price Wars</u>, says our options are clear: "We can defend our price or we can explain our value." Remember, one comes naturally, the former, and the other requires some homework.

Features vs. benefits. Since so many salespeople want to present the features in considerable detail, it must be instinctive. Why else would they do it so often? The facts are easy to discuss because they are so evident. Product features are listed in detail sheets, are given ad nauseaum during training sessions, and are easily recited during a sales call. Benefits, however, must be presented in a way in which they relate to the customer's specific requirements. Benefits create interest by being a significant part of the value chain. Features are logical and benefits are emotional. If you want to become more passionate about your products, don't miss the opportunity to show how each prospect or customer benefits from using your product.

Winging it vs. singing it. The single most important tool a sales person possesses is his words. There are only twenty-six letters in the alphabet, and so many words to choose from, we usually give in to our instincts and confidence to wing our questions and more disturbingly, wing our most common responses. What begins as a comment or response ends up as sales babble. It turns into babble because whenever we don't know exactly what we're going to say, we generally end up saying more than we intended. The best song begins as a selection of words on sheet music. Did you ever wonder how a singer makes a song come alive? The singer studies the words and the music, and then begins singing by matching the words to the rhythm and tempo of the song. Don't wing it, sing it. Make sure your words match your music.

Mental notes vs. written notes. Our basic instinct is to remember important information by making mental notes.

The problem with mental notes is that they aren't always retrievable on demand. How many, "I just remembered I was supposed to . . ." come too late. The sales rep who says, "I keep everything in my head." is fooling himself into thinking he has good notes.

Thirty years ago when life was simpler, you could get away with making mental notes about your prospects and customers. Today, everything is more complicated. Neglecting good notes sends the wrong signal that you don't care. If you care, take notes. If you care a lot, make sure you capture their key words in the form of quotes. Today's street smart salespeople include quotes in their notes.

Improvising vs. preparing. Which is easier to do, improvise or prepare? Naturally, improvising takes less effort. Let's stand in the customer's shoes for a moment. Do you think they can distinguish preparation from improvisation? Of course they can. Preparation isn't an accident. Preparation reveals character. Preparation among salespeople demonstrates uniqueness.

Every road to professionalism is lined with preparation. What should you prepare? Everything!

> **Before everything else, getting ready is the secret of success.**
> **Henry Ford**

> **The future belongs to those who prepare for it.**
> **Ralph Waldo Emerson**

#44

If Business Is Up,
Why Are Salespeople Down?

If business is so good, why are you feeling so bad? To be sure, not everyone is experiencing that sinking feeling. The selling profession is changing dramatically and quickly. If you fail to keep up with the current challenges and changes, it's easy to fall behind and lose your balance.

More than ever, salespeople are experiencing new ways to do their job. Many are self-imposed and some are company imposed. Consider the impact of E-mail and voice mail. Then there is merger mania and acquisition madness. Companies that once had vertical organizations now have paired down horizontal ones. Management sends mixed signals about wanting to increase market share and profitability at the same time. Sales reps receive more product training than they need and less sales training than they require. Most salespeople have more things to do and less time to do them. If you were a car, your instrument panel would be flashing numerous warning lights.

Let's briefly review each of these warning lights.

E-mail. Now this is one nifty concept. First, there's intra-company E-mail allowing us to rapidly communicate with each other. Then, the Internet comes along making it possible for everyone in the entire world to communicate.

If you think twenty to thirty messages a day is a problem, how will you respond to getting hundreds a day? Your junk mail could come via the Internet. Family and friends and even neighbors could flash you a quick note. If you can't deal with today's overload, how are you planning to deal with tomorrow's?

Voice mail. A great idea for some and for others an endless chain of messages that won't go away. Messages can be short. They can be so short and so quick that they must be replayed to be understood. Phone numbers are left without the benefit of the hyphen or pause. Messages can be long and rambling. Messages can be so numerous that your mail box fills up by 9:30 A.M. every day. The heartfelt obligation to return the messages can take as long or longer than it took to replay them.

Merger mania and acquisition madness. I'm convinced that the real losers in the merger and acquisition business are the employees and managers that survive the blood, guts, and termination stuff. When was the last time a survivor was ever told that he'd be getting a hefty increase in salary because he was going to have to work in a chaotic and tumultuous environment and work more hours to handle the work formerly done by three people? Most mergers aren't fun and, according to recent reports, they aren't very successful either.

Horizontal organization charts. Companies are really learning the definition of lean and mean. When a company flattens it's organizational chart it immediately sends a message throughout the company that career opportunities are being reduced accordingly. This affects salespeople and all the people that support salespeople. One of the tragedies of living in these changing times is that we must also contend with lots of people changing jobs both on a voluntary and involuntary basis.

Mixed signals from management. More than ever managers fail to say what they mean and mean what they say. Senior managers insist that five-year strategic plans be prepared annually. Have you ever been in the second year of a five-year plan? Most of us don't get the opportunity because we create new five-year plans every year. It's mindless and senseless, and we still do it. Senior managers often boast that they have an open-door policy. Have you ever tried to get in to see a person who has an open-door policy? It's virtually impossible. Ever hear an executive who said he'll be brief and was? Not on your life. It's all about credibility; you either have it or you don't. It's that simple.

More product training than you need and less sales training than you require. If you're feeling overwhelmed, your company could be partially to blame. A very high percentage of companies that do train their salespeople, limit the training to product training or what to sell. Neanderthal managers really think salespeople need more "what" than "how." That's a concept that is strategically suicidal. Be careful with that one, especially if the competition concentrates on the "how." In the best managed companies, sales training isn't optional.

More things to do and less time to do them. It's a given, there will always be more things to do than time in which to do them. I recently did a seminar for a Chamber of Commerce. There were 250 participants. I asked those who had their written, daily "To Do" list with them to stand. Almost 75% of the group stood. I then asked everyone who didn't have all the calls and all the important things, for that day, on that list to sit. About

30% remained standing. I then asked everyone who didn't have every call and item on that list numbered on a priority basis to sit. Guess how many people remained standing? Just one. In a hotel ballroom containing 250 members of a Chamber of Commerce only one had his day planned on a priority basis. It's not about working hard. Sure there's work to be done and that takes effort. It's about working smart and being effective. In business, not having a prioritized daily "To Do" list, is like being a ship's captain without navigational charts, or a pilot without a compass.

There are 1,440 minutes in every day. You either use them or lose them. Plan your time, and you'll always have enough time to work your plan.

Many salespeople get down. The good ones always get up quickly. Be a rebounder. Rebound quickly and smartly from all the curves tossed your way.

If "True Grit" worked for John Wayne, it may work for you.

Time is the scarcest resource and unless it is managed nothing else can be managed.
Peter Drucker

Tomorrow is often the busiest day of the week.
Anonymous

#45

Small Enough To Care
Big Enough To Perform

If you work for a small company, with sales less than $25 million, you may encounter the "bigger is better" complex. First you get it, than you spread it. Both are big mistakes, that often play to your big competitors' advantage. Here's an example.

One of the big challenges for personnel in the health care industry is the massive consolidation that is taking place. One of my clients, a medical supplies distributor, has experienced considerable consolidation among the physicians' practices. Now, instead of calling on individual doctors, the reps are making sales calls to executives and their committees who manage and control a group of practices. So, what's the problem? The problem is that for some companies it's revolutionizing the selling process. It even has it's own name, called executive selling.

Everyone wants to know how to intelligently approach this new breed of executives, the ones managing big groups. Smaller companies and their representatives often make big concessions, especially when they assume their larger competitors are better positioned and more capable of dealing with larger groups and senior level executives.

Bigger isn't always better. Group executives making group decisions may initially feel larger companies are capable of doing more and costing less. The role of a salesperson in this scenario is to demonstrate that it ain't necessarily so.

Become a farmer. Plant seeds of doubt. Become a spin doctor. Learn to turn things around to your advantage or to your competitor's disadvantage. Once you believe it can be done, it's easy to do.

Our principle tool in developing our approach is choosing the appropriate words. Most uninformed salespeople will do an inadequate job of defending their size. Others will try to sling mud at the competition. A more effective and more subtle approach is to get the prospects or customers to rethink their point of view. It could be one (disturbing) question that you ask, that forces them to think more seriously about your selling proposition.

You could also take a cue from leading advertisers. Look at headlines in print ads. Watch and listen to the verbiage on TV ads. What you'll hear are crisp, clear, and concise words that create mind pictures. Examples include: "We have a better idea." "We try harder."

My client asked me to give them an example. They didn't give me much time to respond. I said, "We're small enough to care and big enough to perform."

Sometimes we're too close to the problem to see the solution. Remember, your perspective is seldom shaped by how close you are to something.

#46

How An Open Mind Unlocks Closed Doors

An "I've always done it this way" attitude isn't the best example of an open mind. Whenever you begin to have these thoughts, it's time to think change. Here are several ideas on how to develop an open mind.

Learning. Go to high school and get a diploma. Go to college and get a degree. Finish with school; know it all and have a degree to prove it. When you combine diminished learning with increased challenges, you get stagnation. Don't let a month go by without reading one business book, one selling magazine, and at least four issues of the Wall Street Journal.

Listening. If you listen to their words, they will buy from you. Hearing your words is less significant than your hearing their words. Listening is a gift, and you must give it to yourself. You are expected to be a good listener, yet are never taught how. When talking to a customer or prospect, always make it a point to get them talking. Two things happen immediately. You'll learn more and the customer will like you better, and that's not a bad trade-off for talking less. The first four letters in the word listen are list. After each sales call, quickly list everything you learned from the call. A long list means something. A short list means something else.

117

Planning. Have a plan and get what you want. Don't have one, and complain about the reasons why. Consider this. Have a map and find your way. Don't have a map, and get lost. Maps show the way, by providing a target and the path. Map your days, your accounts, your territory, your life's goals.

Family. If you want to know how a person spends his money look at his checkbook. If you want to know how a person values his family, check how much time he spends with them. Families are not like savings accounts, you can't save them up expecting a big withdrawal at the end. Whenever possible and practical involve your family in your business. Share the challenges and the rewards.

Retirement. If you want to retire financially secure, there are two numbers that you must become very conversant with. The first number is seventy-two. Actually it's the rule of seventy-two. Any percent return divided into seventy-two will tell you how many years it takes to double your investment. For example a 12% return will double in six years. A 6% percent return will double in twelve years. The next number is ten. Always save at least 10% of your earnings. When you combine 10% savings with the principle of compounding, over an extended period of time great things will always happen. It's called wealth.

All it takes to unlock the door of opportunity is an open mind.

#47

For Example . . .

How would you like to be a one-dimensional sales person? A one-dimensional salesperson discusses facts, mentions specifications, quotes prices, and generally gives a logical, though boring presentation.

You don't have to be a Zig Ziglar to give a passionate and enthusiastic presentation. On the contrary, you can easily create value by choosing your transition words carefully.

For example: try illustrating your key points and relevant topics with examples.

Examples serve two purposes. First and most importantly, they create value. Examples describe, depict, and deliver value in a meaningful way. Second, your examples allow your prospects and customers to experience the value in their preferred style. Some will imagine them, others will hear them, and still others will feel them.

The best way to use examples is when you want to illustrate key points. Here are several examples.

Offer examples when you want to:

- ◼ Describe your customer base
- ◼ Describe how your product works

- Discuss the benefits of using your products.
- Offer a testimonial from a satisfied customer.
- Respond to a customer's questions.
- Handle customer's objections.

If you want to show value, use examples. The mind is like an amusement park, and your words are like the rides. Your words, if carefully prepared, will stir the imagination for even the most hesitant buyer.

Example is a language all men can read.
Anonymous

It's extremely difficult to sell anyone a product you've never used - or a religion you've never lived.
Anonymous

#48

What's The Secret?

The secret is there is no secret to becoming a selling superstar. I've met too many of them to believe that it comes with the genes. Here are some of the characteristics I'm starting to observe in the superstars.

Vision - You are selling myopically if you don't have a written personal vision statement. Additionally, you should be plugged into the firm's vision of the future. Tomorrow's vision is today's agenda. Today is tomorrow's yesterday.

Wizards - Successful salespeople are wizards of something. They may be masters at communicating, maestros of technology, or brilliant with numbers. Whatever it is, they seem to recognize the power of mastery. Mastery isn't a gift. It must be crafted and recrafted to achieve perfection.

Dreamers - Todays best and most professional reps aim high, and set their goals above the horizon. They seldom fear coming up short, what they dread is aiming too low. They dream first and then they prepare goals and pragmatically set out to achieve them within a certain time frame.

Pioneers - Successful salespeople seek out challenges and are the first to embrace change as a positive element in their personal growth and development. They prefer to make tracks than to follow in them. Their least favorite words are "I've always done it this way." Sure they'll think about things, but they spend more time doing than thinking.

Information - Successful salespeople can identify the information they need, know how to get it, and know how to use it. They don't get bogged down with it. You won't find them doing an E-mail, followed by a FAX, and confirmed with a voice mail reminder to be on the look out for both. Time may be our most critical resource, so you can expect the best salespeople to harness the information smorgasbord and resist the temptation to be overwhelmed by it. They have developed strategies to garner and disseminate information in a way that serves their needs best.

Remember, the secret is there is no secret. There is no cookie cutter or one-size fits-all approach to being really successful. Years ago there were many rules to follow. Today, the most important rule may be that there are no rules, just unbelievable opportunities.

> **The price of success is hard work, dedication to the job at hand, and the determination that whether we win or lose, we have applied the best of ourselves to the task at hand.**
> **Vince Lombardi**

#49

Prospecting The New-Fashioned Way

There is one thing that inhibits the development of new business, it's inadequate prospecting. It goes by other names, the most common is cold-calling. Imagine being asked to do something as important as bringing in new business and referring to it as cold-calling. Both terms, prospecting and cold-calling are old-fashioned and out dated. It is more appropriate to refer to this strategically important part of selling as networking, base-building, or managing the pipeline. You will achieve new sales growth either from existing customers or new ones.

Now that we can call it by another name, how do we do it? I'd like to say it's easy, but it isn't. It involves hard work and smart work. Here are several ideas, designed to trigger additional ones. Before you say it won't work in your business, think how it might be adapted.

Here's one from an advertising agency in Florida. With a targeted account in mind, walk into an office just before lunch time with a customerized box of pizza. People will smell it and it will get to the right person. Scott Jackson, founder of Jackson Design Group, delivers the pizza with one slice missing. In the open space it says, "For a larger slice of your market, call Jackson Design." Half of the pizza recipients signed up with the agency.

Another group of entrepreneurs sent baby booties to prospective clients with a note saying they just wanted to "get a foot in the door." Informal networking can also work. Set up a monthly breakfast meeting with other salespeople. You can share selling ideas and experiences as well as new account contacts.

I've saved the best for last. Nothing beats a great referral. That's the good news. The bad news is that few salespeople know how to ask. Sure, there is the old stand-by, "Do you know anybody who might be interested?" Be honest with yourself. How many referrals do you get with that approach?

Referrals are a geometric alternative to building your business. If you can secure one solid referral a week, imagine what the impact would be on your business. I've developed a proven approach to securing new referrals. If you're interested, send me your business card with your referral technique written on the back. I'll be happy to share my ideas with you just for the asking.

What you did last year means less than what you'll do this year. Building a new business that grows every year takes a unique effort to bring in new customers. Whether you call it networking, base-building, or managing the pipeline isn't the issue. Attracting new customers is. You either know how to do it or you don't.

> **Creative activity is one of the few self rewarding activities. Being creative is like being in love!**
>
> **Woody Flowers**

#50

Fifty And Still Going

Well, I may not be going as fast as the Duracell battery, but I'm still going. I still have dreams and plans. The work I do is challenging, and I love doing it. The highest compliment I've ever received, is being called a teacher. Being a teacher has made me a better student. I've learned more in the last eight years than during the first forty-two.

In their book, <u>If It Ain't Broke . . . Break It</u>, Robert Kriegel and Louis Patler uncovered some rather interesting information. A team of researchers followed a group of 1,500 people over a period of twenty years. At the outset of the study, the participants were divided into two groups, Group A and Group B.

Group A, which composed 83% percent of the sample, were people who were embarking on a career path that they had chosen solely for the prospect of making money now in order to do what they wanted later in life.

Group B, the other 17% of the sample, consisted of people who had chosen their career paths so they could do what they wanted to do now and worry about the money later.

The data showed some startling revelations: At the end of the twenty-year period, 101 of the 1,500 had become millionaires.

Of the 101 millionaires, 100 were from group B, the group that had chosen to pursue what they loved.

The key ingredient in most successful careers is the passion and love the people bring to their jobs. Having a goal or a plan is not enough. Academic preparation is not enough. Prior experience is not enough. Enjoyment of life's work is the key.

Chasing the dollar isn't where it's at. Find something you really enjoy doing and the compensation will surely follow. Life is far too short to spend all those years, months, and endless hours doing work you don't like.

If you don't like your work - leave it. Don't rationalize away the rest of your life saying you're doing it for the money. Leaving a secure job with a guaranteed, weekly paycheck may be the biggest risk you've ever taken as it was for me. But if you identify your love and develop it into a career, the results will be gratifying and financially rewarding.

If it can work for me, it certainly can work for you.

Let me tell you something, kid. If you can fall in love with what you're going to do for a living, you got it made. I fell in love with show business about 90 years ago, and I love it just as much today. And that's the truth.

George Burns

Resources

Success Magazine
800-234-7324

Selling Power
800-752-7355

Selling
800-360-5344

Sales & Marketing Management
800-821-6897

Telephone Selling Report
402-895-9399

The Competitive Advantage
800-722-9221

Nightingale-Conant Audio Tapes
800-525-9000

Product List

Books: $19.95

#1	<u>47 Ways To Sell Smarter</u>
#2	<u>50 More Ways To Sell Smarter</u>

Audio Cassettes: $19.95

#3	"How To Win More Sales"
#4	"The Ten Best Questions To Ask Customers"
#5	"Maximum Results In Minimum Time"
#6	"How To Double Your Business Without Quadrupling Your Effort"
#7	"Closing The Sale"

Newsletter: $39.00

#8	<u>Sales Strategist</u> (three issues per year)

Selling Reports: $4.50

#9	"How To Watch Your Time & Grow Your Territory"
#10	"Twelve Ways To Create A Personal Selling Edge"

Special Deals For Multiple Orders

#11	Any combination of 5 books and/or tapes = $70
#12	Any combination of 4 books and/or tapes = $60
#13	Any combination of 3 books and/or tapes = $49

Mail or FAX Order Form

Mail: JM Associates
         824 Paddock Lane, Libertyville, IL 60048
FAX: 847-680-7881

Please rush me:

Item #	Unit Price	Quantity	Total

SUBTOTAL

TAX (IL residents add 6.5%)

SHIPPING & HANDLING: (add $2/tape
and $2/book and $.50/selling report)

Total

Name_____Company _____

Address_____

City/State/Zip_____

Phone_____FAX_____

_____ **Check or Money Order (payable to JM Associates)**

_____ **Credit Card: Visa   Master Card (circle one)**
        Account Number_____
        Exp. Date_____

_____ **Purchase Order #**_____
        Accepted for orders over $200